The Musical Experience

The Musical Experience:

Sound, Movement, and Arrival

Leonard G. Ratner

W.H. Freeman and Company
New York   San Francisco

This book was published originally as a part of *The Portable Stanford*, a series of books published by the Stanford Alumni Association, Stanford, California.

Library of Congress Cataloging in Publication Data

Ratner, Leonard G.
  The musical experience.

  Reprint. Originally published: Stanford, Calif.:
Stanford Alumni Association, 1983. (The Portable
Stanford)
  Includes index.
  1. Music appreciation.   2. Musical analysis.
3. Musical form. I. Title. II. Series: Portable
Stanford.
MT6.R24M88 1983   780'.1'5   83-5501
ISBN 0-7167-1475-2
ISBN 0-7167-1476-0 (pbk.)

Printed in the United States of America

9 8 7 6 5 4 3 2 1 CP 1 0 8 9 8 7 6 5 4 3

CONTENTS

PREFACE

MUSIC IS A RICH AND VARIED ART. It offers something of value to each of us. It moves us; it stirs our feelings. When we say, "Listen to that beat!" or, "I like that sound!" we touch upon the essence of music: its power to affect us.

This book begins where you as a listener begin—with how music sounds, how it moves, and where it is going. Sound affects us immediately; it is our first contact with what the music has to say. It creates a mood: a low sound may make you feel comfortable, sober, or sad, while a high sound may command your attention or raise your spirits. When sound moves it conveys an impression of action—slow, fast, gentle, vigorous. Like sound, movement makes an immediate impression on a listener. Movement is going somewhere, and when it arrives we know that one action is completed and a new start can be made. Listening for musical sound, movement, and arrival can give you a vivid idea of what a piece of music is saying and how it takes shape as it proceeds.

Throughout this book, sound, movement, and arrival form the basic criteria for listening to music. First, these criteria are explained in everyday, nontechnical language and illustrated with examples from familiar concert music. Then, with that basis, we explore the language of music—its rhythm, melody, harmony, texture, and form. We see that music is an orderly art. Its processes fit together with the precision and elegance of a fine watch. This orderliness can help you as a listener sort out the relationships within a musical composition. When you fix your attention on a prominent feature in the music—a specific quality of sound, a pattern of movement, or the way it arrives—you can see how the action arranges itself around this feature, much as a magnet will draw iron filings to itself. Finally, we bring both the basic criteria and the language of music together for a look at the ways several masterworks have been formed.

The approach of this book is to let you be friends with music. The book moves in easy steps from general ideas of musical expression to elements of its language to great works of musical art. At any point you may pause, yet still have a coherent idea of the musical experience.

From the vast repertory of concert music I have chosen a small group of works as principal sources for examples. These come mainly from eighteenth- and nineteenth-century music. The musical language of that period is no doubt already familiar to you, and you may know some of these particular compositions. Excerpts from many of them (arranged for piano) are recorded on the soundsheets accompanying this book. To get an even more vivid image of these works, you will find it helpful as well as enjoyable to listen to the complete original works beforehand, then return to them in the course of your reading. They are:

Bach:	Mass in B Minor, "Crucifixus," "Et Resurrexit"
Bach:	*The Well-Tempered Clavier*, Book I, Fugues nos. 1 (C major) and 2 (C minor)
Bartók:	*Music for String Instruments, Percussion, and Celesta*
Beethoven:	Symphony no. 3 in E♭ Major (*Eroica*), Op. 55
Beethoven:	Symphony no. 5 in C Minor, Op. 67
Berlioz:	*Symphonie Fantastique*
Brahms:	Symphony no. 1 in C Minor, Op. 68
Tchaikovsky:	*The Nutcracker* Suite
Chopin:	Prelude no. 4 in E Minor
Liszt:	Sonata in B Minor for Piano
Mendelssohn:	Music for *A Midsummer Night's Dream*
Mozart:	Don Giovanni
Mozart:	Sonata in A Major, K. 331
Schubert:	"The Erlking"
Schubert:	"The Linden Tree"
Stravinsky:	*Le Sacre du Printemps*
Wagner:	*Tristan and Isolde,* Prelude and "Liebestod"

In addition to the works listed above, quotations from other compositions appear in the musical examples to illustrate specific points. All the examples have been arranged so that you can play them with ease at the piano. (Musical examples recorded on the soundsheets are indicated by * in their headings. Some examples appear more than once in the book. The headings of those examples will refer you to the number by which they are recorded on the soundsheets.)

This book is intended for the lay person who wishes to sharpen his or her listening focus in order to enrich the listening experience. All that is described and explained here has but one aim: to help illuminate and enrich your personal listening experience.

I wish to thank the following persons who participated in the preparation of this book: John Boykin, for his careful and perceptive editing; Josephine Gandolfi, for performing the musical examples on the sound-sheets; Jonathan Berger, for preparing numerous musical examples in the text using the computer music printing system of Leland Smith and the San Andreas Press. I should also like to express my appreciation to the publications staff of the Stanford Alumni Association for their enthusiastic encouragement at all stages in the production of this book.

Leonard G. Ratner

Stanford, California
May 1, 1983

Marcel Marceau.

1

Musical Expression

SUPPOSE YOU AND A FEW FRIENDS, after listening to Mendelssohn's Overture to *A Midsummer Night's Dream*, compare your responses to the music. If you reflect on what you enjoyed most in the piece, you might say that it has colorful sounds, that it moves lightly, that it suggests an image of a midnight elfin scamper, or that it is beautifully put together. Each of you might be more impressed by one feature than by another, yet you would probably all agree that this is a very playful piece.

These responses reflect two basic aspects of the musical experience: the personal and the general. As in any language, they combine. Your personal experience in music draws upon terms, procedures, and attitudes that listeners generally understand and that composers put into fresh formulations in each new piece of music. As listeners we also sense music in general ways. We sense the climate created by sounds themselves. We sense the way music moves and builds shapes and the way it stirs feelings and inspires certain moods. We may also perceive musical associations with poetry, drama, and dance that suggest images. From these general aspects we draw our personal responses.

Music as Climate

For a composer, the simplest way to create an effect is to establish a climate of sound. Mendelssohn prepares his listeners for an adventure on a balmy night in midsummer by filling the air with light and bright sounds—some sustained, some piquant and flickering. Wagner sets the tragic climate of his music-drama *Tristan and Isolde* with dark, heavy, colorful sounds. Beethoven, at the beginning of his Symphony no. 6, the *Pastoral*, uses a quiet, murmuring sound effect to tell his listeners that he is in the country. On another scale, background music such as Muzak creates a climate just by being played. It establishes a continual presence. It creates a minor magic, a lightly enveloping touch that removes us from a matter-of-fact mood. All music creates its own climate. Whether you are encountering a piece of music for the first time or exploring it more deeply on subsequent hearings, you may very well get an idea what the composer wants to say just by concentrating on the climate of sound he creates at the very beginning.

Music as Gesture

Rise, fall; quick, slow; straight, bent; long, short; flowing, broken; gentle, vigorous—these are some of the shapes and motions that music can create. Think of them as gestures. For us as listeners, these gestures stir inner responses, such as growing tension, release, excitement, serenity.

They can also communicate in a pantomimic way. For example, Beethoven begins his Symphony no. 3, the *Eroica*, with two massive strokes that command our attention, then he presents the smooth and undulating tune, and follows with a slight but disturbing sag in the line. He eventually restores a sense of firmness, but only after weaving a complex web of falling and rising gestures. With this interplay of gestures Beethoven alerts us to the broadly gauged, tightly spun action that will ensue throughout the movement. Similarly, the short, neatly patterned gestures Mozart places at the opening of his *Eine kleine Nachtmusik* bespeak the playfulness that characterizes the piece.

Music as Association

Most of the music we hear nowadays carries associations with some scene, action, object, or with words or pictures. Television commercials reinforce their selling point by fitting music to message. Movies use music to guide your feelings according to the way the plot unfolds. In much the same way, Mendelssohn, setting out to write music for *A Midsummer Night's Dream*, took his cue from Shakespeare's fairy tale—the play of sprites, the sentimental mood of night, the joy of the wedding.

Composers sometimes pinpoint their musical associations. Prokofieff identifies each character and action in *Peter and the Wolf* with an appropriate musical fragment—for example, the quacking duck described by the oboe, or Peter's jauntiness suggested in a march tune played by the clarinet. Haydn depicts the opening chapters of Genesis in *The Creation* by describing wind, water, light, dark, rivers, rain, trees, flowers, and all manner of birds, reptiles, and mammals with appropriate musical figures.

Associations can also be quite subtle. For example, to wind up the first act of *The Marriage of Figaro*, Mozart has Figaro march the obstreperous Cherubino (who has been assigned to army duty) around the stage in a mock military march. The march itself, while it has a few hints of battle music along the way, is set in a light, elegant manner—almost as toy music. You can associate this music both with Cherubino's playfulness and with the cavalier he is to become.

Music as Feeling

The power of music to stir the feelings is actually at the center of the musical experience. This power is the reason music is more art than science. The range of feeling music can express is broad—from the mournful funeral march which constitutes the second movement of Beethoven's Symphony no. 3 to the exuberant "Wedding March" from Mendelssohn's *Midsummer Night's Dream* music.

In between there are of course innumerable nuances. In music set to a text you can pinpoint the emotion, such as the terror in the child's outcry, "My father, my father," when he feels the menace of the specter of death in Schubert's song "The Erlking." In music without text, nuances of feeling can be conveyed instrumentally, as when a violin or a flute swells on a tone to create an instant of urgency. At a climactic moment in Wagner's *Tristan and Isolde,* the music sweeps you up into a powerful tide of sensation. On the other hand, Bach distills emotion in his music so that as it proceeds you sense the feeling within the fascinating play of sound and movement.

It is perfectly natural for two listeners to react to the same work in different ways. No reaction is better or worse than another, for none is right or wrong. Feeling is the truly personal part of the musical experience, in which you, the listener, have the final word.

Music as Design

Musical design is the composer's plan, whereby he sustains feeling and gives it time to run its course. Design puts musical climate, gestures, and associations into effective patterns that build the form of a piece. For example, in the Overture to *A Midsummer Night's Dream* Mendelssohn prolongs the opening sounds to establish a climate of sound, spins out the scampering figures by repeating and varying them, interrupts the play strategically by a recall of the sustained notes, then resumes the play. This is musical design at work, much like in a fine piece of sculpture or a Greek temple.

Design can do two things. It can connect and it can separate. Mendelssohn creates a broad arch of connection in his overture by ending it with the same distinctive, evocative sounds with which he began. Also, moment to moment throughout the piece, you can hear how skillfully he dovetails one passage into another. This is also connection. On a much simpler scale, Beethoven gave the "Ode to Joy" in his Ninth Symphony a smooth flow by connecting its notes in unbroken upward

Muscular Dynamism by Umberto Boccioni, 1913, charcoal drawing, 34″ × 23¼″. Collection, The Museum of Modern Art, New York. Given anonymously.

and downward motion. Design also separates. Through stops and starts or through effective changes of manner—gentle to forceful, for example—it helps you maintain your bearings within a piece. Each part of the Mendelssohn overture, although neatly fitted into the overall scheme of the piece, has its own character. So the interplay of connection and separation is essential in musical design.

As we proceed to look deeper into these elements of the musical experience, we shall first see how they contribute to musical expression, then examine some of the processes by which these elements come into being. Finally we shall see how design contributes to the final perfection of a work of musical art.

Swan by Henri Matisse, 1930–32, etching, 13″ × 9¾″. Collection, The Museum of Modern Art, New York. Mrs. John D. Rockefeller Jr. Purchase fund.

2

Sound as Expression

SOUND TOUCHES US. Physically, as vibration in the air, it stirs the sense of hearing. Metaphorically, as a signal, it awakens our feelings. Sound commands our attention and holds it. For example, play a single note on the piano, perhaps middle C, using the sustaining pedal. As the silence is broken, the tone takes your attention; as you try to hear the fading tone, your concentration is intensified.

We all recognize basic qualities of sound—pitch, strength, amount, and color—even if some of the terms are unfamiliar. In a casual way we can say, "This sound is low, that sound is soft, this sound is full, that sound is rich." By describing sounds in this way we make some simple but useful evaluations. Beyond this point, we may ask, "What is the effect of this low sound, that soft tone, this fullness, that richness?" In other words, "Why did the composer choose these qualities from among all that he had available, and to what expressive purpose?" Most important: "How persuasive do we find these choices?"

Pitch

Pitch is how high or how low a note sounds. The level of pitch at which a musical passage is set affects the impression of mood. We tend to associate levels of pitch with degrees of buoyancy or heaviness. For instance, Mendelssohn begins the Overture to his music for *A Midsummer Night's Dream* on a high level of pitch to give us an impression of the lightness and agility of Puck, the wood sprite, and of his elfin cohorts. Franz Liszt probes the lower depths of pitch to begin his Sonata in B Minor, thereby establishing the moods of introspection and great portent that pervade this piece. Brahms covers the entire range of sound to create a massive, grandiose effect at the beginning of his Symphony no. 1—an opening proper for a piece in a heroic vein.

Much music, including familiar songs and dances, remains on a middle level of pitch. In such cases, we listen for other elements, such as musical color or motion. In a few striking instances, the composer combines extremes of high and low pitches without a binder in the middle. Béla Bartók evokes a strange and elusive mood in this manner at the beginning of the third movement of his *Music for String Instruments, Percussion, and Celesta;* he places disembodied tones at a great distance from each other, with nothing intervening.

Composers deploy changes in pitch level to help give shape to a piece. Wagner, in the Prelude to *Tristan and Isolde,* builds steadily to an extreme of high pitch to convey an impression of the increasing emotional tension that carries through the opera itself. Bach, in his familiar Prelude in C Major from the *Well-Tempered Clavier,* Book I, reaches a high point in the melody very quickly and then, for the rest of the piece, moves steadily downward in subsiding waves of rise and fall in pitch.

Strength and Amount

Strength of sound—the degree of loudness—also has great power to convey expressive values. Loud music tends to pound on us; soft music moves us with persuasion. A marked increase in strength (called crescendo) gives the impression of growing tension, as in the most celebrated example, Ravel's *Bolero.* He builds the entire piece upon an unrelenting increase to convey the effect of excitement that finally reaches the point of frenzy. A gradual decrease in strength (called decrescendo) has the opposite effect: relaxation or release. Tchaikovsky, by gradually decreasing the strength and amount of sound at the end of his Symphony no. 6, conveys a mood of utter despair and resignation.

Composers prescribe strength of sound to performers by using certain conventional signs and terms, collectively called dynamics:

ppp	pianississimo	extremely soft
pp	pianissimo	very soft
p	piano	soft
mp	mezzo piano	moderately soft
mf	mezzo forte	moderately full or loud
f	forte	strong or loud
ff	fortissimo	very loud
fff	fortississimo	extremely loud

Sometimes, to dramatize their point, composers have written "pppp" or "ffff" to indicate the utter extremes of soft or loud in their music.

We can easily tell the difference between various amounts of sound. A large mass of sound, with many performers chiming in, has a powerful impact; a small amount conveys a lighter effect. Try to imagine a piece such as the "Hallelujah Chorus" from Handel's *Messiah* being sung with only one voice or one instrument to a part. The original impression of majesty and grandeur would shrink to thinness and transparency. For each participant in the musical experience—the composer, the performer, the listener—the amount of sound employed is critical in the proper projection of musical expression.

Dynamic changes can be minute, adding expressive nuances to a musical performance. Very often the difference between a moving performance and a dull one is the degree of shading which the master artist uses to shape a passage, the slight swellings and taperings of sound which place the musical effects in clear and meaningful perspective. This can be overdone; nevertheless, when projected with subtlety and taste, it is one of the delights of the musical experience.

Tone Color (Timbre)

Unlike pitch, amount, and strength, tone color (or *timbre*) cannot easily be measured or defined. Our perception of tone color is rather like our sense of taste. A common flavor can be sweet, salty, sour, bland, spicy, rich, or thin. But more specialized flavors elude such simple descriptions; they must be experienced to be recognized and appreciated. Tone color, like taste, has some general values. It may be bright, as at the beginning of Mendelssohn's Overture to *A Midsummer Night's Dream*; it may be dark, as at the beginning of Tchaikovsky's Symphony no. 6; it may be thin, as at the beginning of Igor Stravinsky's *L'Histoire du Soldat*; it may be rich, as at the beginning of Brahms's Symphony no. 1.

The richest and most varied palette of tone color is offered by the symphony orchestra. Since the early eighteenth century the strings—violin, viola, violoncello, and contrabass—have been the mainstay of the orchestra, establishing its core of sound. We all recognize the sound of strings—clear and bright in the upper ranges, mellow to dark in the lower ranges. The other orchestral groups—woodwinds, brass, and percussion—became prominent in the nineteenth century when the instruments' mechanical features were perfected to achieve agility as well as richness of tone. Composers took full advantage of such technical improvements to extend their musical expression.

Tone colors, like colors in painting, are highlighted by being set against each other. Therefore, to enjoy the full flavor of the colors modern orchestral instruments can produce, listen for them in a complete piece. Two works that exploit this aspect of musical sound very imaginatively are Berlioz's *Symphonie Fantastique* and Tchaikovsky's *Nutcracker* Suite.

In the "Miniature Overture" of the *Nutcracker* Suite, Tchaikovsky gives the piccolo a prominent role. As the piece builds in amount and strength toward its end, the piercing tone of this highest of the woodwinds adds a touch of frenzy to the general excitement. Trumpets set the military mood of the "March" with their crisp, clear tones. Tchaikovsky plays the game of contrast most effectively in the "Dance of the Sugar Plum Fairy" as he answers the gentle bell-like sounds of the celesta with the dark, low, somewhat hollow sound of the bass clarinet. In the "Danse Arabe" clarinets and English horn provide a somewhat melancholy effect as they play in their low registers. The flute whirls around in its most brilliant register in the "Chinese Dance," accompanied by a steady pulse of short, plump notes in the lower register of the bassoon. Glittering harp and mellow horn join to finish this musical feast with a rich confection in the "Waltz of the Flowers."

Tchaikovsky, in his play of tone color, clearly aims to please; Berlioz, in his *Symphonie Fantastique*, aims to surprise. While his effects of tone color have polish, they often make their points with contrast and the unexpected. Berlioz brings in the contrabass at one point in the introduction to the first movement, plucking out a solo melody while the upper instruments have virtually nothing to say. At the beginning of the third movement he creates a pastoral duet between the English horn and the oboe, setting off each instrument as a solo. Their somewhat edgy, penetrating sounds—the oboe clearer than the dark English horn—give the feeling of loneliness and distance, of the open space associated with a pastoral mood. At the end of this movement the timpani, in an imitation of thunder, stir four different but indistinct pitches to give a totally murky effect of tone color. Trombones—instruments traditionally associated with authority—lend their heavy sound to the sentence of death as the "March to the Scaffold" approaches its climax. In the finale, the "Witches Sabbath," Berlioz assembles a collage of weird color effects, starting with the veil of sound that the strings draw at the opening, through the shrill antics of the clarinets and the burbling of the bassoons in a grotesque dance, to the doomsday tolling of bells and finally the announcement of the "Dies Irae" ("Day of Wrath") in ponderous, muffled tones by the tubas.

Tchaikovsky and Berlioz link their play of tone color to specific stories. Mozart, on the other hand, creates something of a pictorial effect without spelling out any story line at the beginning of his *Prague* Symphony by a series of short, contrasted bits of tone color. A knowledgeable listener in Mozart's time would recognize these kaleidoscopic fragments as having been drawn from operatic scenes of the supernatural, where ghosts and gods appear.

Harmonic Color

Notes sounding at the same time create their own effects of color. Some groups of notes have a sweet sound that seems nicely blended and stable. Other combinations sound harsh and quite unstable, as if the tones were rejecting each other. These properties of note combinations constitute harmonic color.

Harmonic color is a fundamental feature of any musical idiom because it helps us recognize immediately the kind of message the composer is communicating in the music. For example, in music written for religious purposes around the tenth century, the harmonic color typically consisted of what we call open or hollow sounds. Because these are particularly resonant, they reverberated dramatically throughout the stone churches as groups of worshippers sang them. Example 2-1 illustrates this kind of rather heavy sound. Listen to it on the soundsheet and try to imagine men's voices singing it slowly in a cloister, as an intoned prayer. (If you are not familiar with musical notation, see the Appendix, "How to Read Music.")

* EXAMPLE 2-1   Medieval harmony.

Later, Renaissance composers learned to link fuller and richer combinations very smoothly. When you listen to Renaissance music, observe how full and balanced the sounds are and how they flow one into the other, without marked change of color. Renaissance music owes much of its elegance and suaveness to this refined treatment of harmonic color (Example 2-2).

* EXAMPLE 2-2   Renaissance harmony.

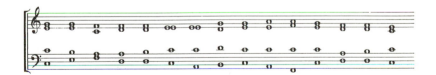

While they used much the same grouping of notes that Renaissance composers employed, later composers turned them to different color effects and expressive content. Beethoven, to open the finale of his Symphony no. 5, uses the same tones that we hear at the beginning of

Example 2-2, but he gives them to the entire orchestra to create a massive and brilliant color. He hammers home the effect by great fullness and strength of sound (Example 2-3).

* EXAMPLE 2-3   Classic harmony. Beethoven: Symphony no. 5.

In music of the middle and late nineteenth century, composers developed, along with a richer and more varied palette of instrumental color, a more intense and colorful effect of harmony. Wagner was the composer who did the most to establish this kind of color as the prevailing harmonic climate of the time. He saturated his music-dramas with the kinds of sound that you hear in Example 2-4. Imagine them performed by instruments that combine to produce a luxurious swell of sound—massed winds, low strings, horns, and trombones.

* EXAMPLE 2-4   Romantic harmony. Typical chords in Wagner's vocabulary.

unstable intervals marked

Music in the twentieth century has retained much of the color of earlier harmony. This is true of popular music, musical comedy, and music for radio and television, as well as a considerable amount of concert music written since 1900. Many composers, however, have explored the possibilities of new harmonic effects. They have removed the core of sound, the full mix of notes that gives a chord blend and solidity. If you imagine the tones in Example 2-5 (already separated widely in pitch) played by instruments of markedly different color (oboe, violin, and horn, for example), you will get the unblended effect that characterizes much music of our present age.

* EXAMPLE 2-5   Twentieth-century harmony.

Electronics have added a new and formidable dimension to our musical experience. Apart from the increasingly faithful reproduction of instrumental and vocal sound, electronics can modify natural sounds in countless ways to create effects absolutely unprecedented in our experience. Electronics can also create sounds directly from electronic sources, without recourse to natural sounds. The composer-synthesizer has absolute control over pitch and duration of notes, down to the most minute microscale—much more than a live performer has. The new music is not well represented in concert halls, but you probably have encountered it as background music for television programs and motion pictures, particularly those on science fiction themes.

Tightrope Walker by Paul Klee, 1923, transfer lithograph, 17⅛″ × 10⅝″. Collection, The Museum of Modern Art, New York. Given anonymously.

3

Movement as Expression

WHILE SOUND TOUCHES US, musical movement invites us to take part. We tap our feet to music, we nod our heads, we may even sway and dance to it. In a sense, musical movement mirrors life itself. Breathing, growing, the change of day to night—these are motions by which we live. Musical movement also reflects the ebb and flow of our feelings and moods. Our physical and emotional responses to the movement of music are touched off by its pace, its regularity, its force, and its flow.

Pace of Movement: Tempo

Tap your finger on a tabletop and you create movement. Tap slowly and you create one kind of pace; tap quickly and you create another kind of pace. What sort of expression can you convey with this bare-bones kind of movement? Well, with just a dash of imagination, you might sense a reflective mood, perhaps melancholy or even a tragic vein in your slow taps. With your quick taps, you might suggest excitement, elation, fury, perhaps anxiety. Mix slow taps with quick taps and you can convey an effect of questioning, of tension.

Tempo is the term that denotes pace of movement. Composers use traditional Italian terms, as a rule, to tell the performer what degree of quickness or slowness to take. They often rely on the same terms to indicate expression. Thus Mozart, in one of his most poignant musical statements, the second movement of his Concerto in A Major, simply prescribes *andante* as the tempo. This is a moderately slow tempo. Beethoven, in the second movement of his Quartet in F Major, has music move at about the same basic pace as Mozart's, yet Beethoven's tempo instructions are much more precise: *adagio affettuoso ed appassionato* (very slowly, affectively and passionately). Mozart expected the performers to take their expressive cues from the music itself; Beethoven directed his performers to take an expressive stance.

The spectrum of tempo moves from *largo* (broad) and *grave* (solemn), the slowest of tempos, to *vivace* (lively) and *presto* (very fast), the quickest of tempos. In between we have *adagio* and *lento* (slow), *andante* (moderately slow), *allegretto* (moderately quick), and *allegro* (quick). Examples of these tempos are:

> *Largo:* Berlioz, *Symphonie Fantastique,* introduction
> *Grave:* Handel, *Messiah,* overture
> *Adagio:* Berlioz, *Symphonie Fantastique,* third movement
> *Lento:* Stravinsky, *Le Sacre du Printemps,* beginning
> *Andante:* Mozart, *Eine kleine Nachtmusik,* second movement
> *Allegretto:* Beethoven, Symphony no. 7, second movement
> *Allegro:* Beethoven, Symphony no. 5, finale
> *Vivace:* Beethoven, Symphony no. 7, finale
> *Presto:* Haydn, Symphony no. 102, finale

Another way to denote tempo is by means of the metronome, which works either mechanically with a pendulum or electrically. Setting a metronome to register a given number of ticks per minute establishes a regular pulse; in this way a composer can prescribe a precise tempo. Bartók, in this century, was fastidious: he took advantage of both the terminology and the metronome. Thus, for the first movement of his *Music for String Instruments, Percussion, and Celesta,* he indicates a style, *andante tranquillo,* and an exact pulse, 112 to 116 eighth notes per minute. As the movement proceeds, Bartók varies the number of eighth notes per minute according to the same kind of precise measurements. He makes such changes in speed throughout the four movements of this work, without necessarily modifying the quality of feeling that rules each movement.

Regularity of Movement

Regularity of movement refers to the extent to which music maintains a given pace. To experience regularity and its disturbance, tap your finger again. Begin a series of taps, about two taps per second. Keep doing this for twenty to thirty seconds. As you continue your mind will begin to wander, because regularity, undisturbed, tends to recede into the background of your attention. Next experiment: after about eight or nine taps, strike one with more force, then resume your normal tapping; a bit later, close the time gap between two or three taps; then stretch one single tap to a full second or two. You and anyone else listening will begin to focus on that play of time and on the emphasis in the series of taps—some message, with expressive potential, is being delivered.

Finally, make a random series of taps, taking care to avoid regularity or repetition of patterns. A listener would yield totally to the whim of your improvisation. Perhaps something striking would be communicated from instant to instant, but the listener's attention, held so tightly, would soon become fatigued.

These three processes—regularity, calculated disturbance, and randomness—represent the composer's fundamental techniques for managing musical movement. Of these, calculated disturbance is by far the most intriguing, and offers the greatest range of effects. Examples of each process abound in our repertory of listening. Sousa's great march, "The Stars and Stripes Forever," maintains an underlying regularity, as does most dance or march music or music set to poetry. Calculated irregularities abound in the first movement of Beethoven's Symphony no. 3; their role is to create a whiplash effect, a momentary imbalance which reinforces the return to regular motion. Much of the expressive impact of Beethoven's music arises from his matchless control of calculated irregularities in movement.

Total irregularity—that is, music that seems to have no underlying pulse to control movement—is prominent in today's avant-garde styles. Such music is either based on chance or controlled to the nth degree by means of computer techniques. Karlheinz Stockhausen used such apparently random methods in his *Gesang der Jünglinge* (Song of the Youths). In the standard repertoire, the opening of Stravinsky's *Le Sacre du Printemps* has a wandering, irregular quality of movement, while the beginning of the finale of Berlioz's *Symphonie Fantastique* pieces together differing bits of movement to reinforce the grotesquerie that characterizes the "Dream of a Witches' Sabbath."

Brahms joins different kinds of movement magnificently as his Symphony no. 1 in C Minor gets under way. The foundation of the complex interplay is the steady, powerful pulse in the lowermost instruments. Above this rocklike support, two different lines of action criss-cross: a steady and slow descent moves against an irregular rising stream of very long and very short notes.

Force and Flow of Movement

Two pieces may proceed at the same pace, but one will sound gentle and the other vehement according to the intensity the performers convey. In a given piece, the force of movement can change the meaning of an idea. For example, toward the end of the first movement of his Symphony no. 3, Beethoven reintroduces the familiar opening theme gently in the violins. He then repeats it three times, gradually building. By the fourth statement, it has become a forceful, victorious shout by the brass and winds.

Martha Graham Dance Troupe performing *Night Journey.*

Flow of movement simply refers to the continuity of sound in music. When the sounds connect without the slightest interruption, the flow is unbroken. When there is an instant of silence between notes, the flow is broken. For example, if you should hum the "Ode to Joy" from Beethoven's Symphony no. 9, you would connect (slur) the tones. This manner is called *legato.* On the other hand, if you tap out the notes of this tune, each tap would be separated from its neighbors. This manner of performance is called *détaché* or in even more marked separations, *staccato.* Stravinsky makes an extreme use of *détaché* in the opening piece of *L'Histoire du Soldat,* with its puppet-show scene, its wryly humorous grotesquerie, and its skeletal scoring. In sharp contrast, a virtually pure *legato* fuses the melodies of Gregorian chant, the ancient music of the Catholic church. Here voices move smoothly and deliberately to express profound feelings.

Each style period had typical qualities of movement in its music. Medieval music, as represented by Gregorian chant, moved gently. Depending on the nature of the piece, it moved with the free declamation of speech or with the regularity of a poetic meter—rather like our *andante.* Renaissance composers established a steady and moderate pulse with a connected flow in their vocal music. Their instrumental music had more marked accentuation and often incorporated rushes of very quick notes over the steady pulse. Throughout the Baroque period, the pace ranged from quite slow to very quick and from irregular to vigorously regular, reflecting the wide range of expression represented in its repertory. Classic composers retained these qualities and increased the range of force, from very light-footed motion to powerful action. Romantic composers, enchanted by the richer sounds of the newly improved piano, the expanded orchestra, and a fantastically colored harmonic palette, tended to slow action so the listener could savor momentary effects or remain within a given mood. At the other extreme, they sometimes wrote incredibly quick music to display the superhuman skills of the hero–virtuosi who dominated nineteenth-century musical performance. With the exception of a few flamboyant composers—Berlioz, Liszt, Wagner—Romantic composers tended to frame their effects in a pace that was even more regular than that of their Classic predecessors. In the present century, composers have used all kinds of movement. The powerful percussion of rock and the totally unaccented effects of much avant-garde music represent extremes in qualities of movement. They explore areas of experience that were unknown in previous music. Like the new sounds of our time, they can become resources to enrich the mainstream of Western music.

Riding School by Franz Marc, 1913, woodcut, 10⅝″ × 11½″. Collection, The Museum of Modern Art, New York. Gift of Abby Aldrich Rockefeller.

4

Arrival: The Shape of Music

MUSIC MOVES TOWARD GOALS. To be intelligible, musical movement must arrive, and any action that throws musical movement into relief provides you with a sense of arrival. For example, the tone of an electric motor has a certain musical quality—a steady pitch and perhaps even a pleasant *timbre*. As it hums along monotonously, though, you quickly tune it out as meaningless background noise. But suppose the hum stops for a second or two, then resumes. For that moment, your attention is fixed on the effect produced by the silence. That silence acts as a point of arrival for the moving sound of the motor. Now, suppose the motor speeds up and the pitch rises. Again, your attention is fixed, drawn to the onset of the higher pitch as a point of arrival. These two points of arrival might be illustrated graphically, as in Example 4-1.

EXAMPLE 4-1

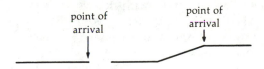

In a composition, points of arrival form a chain that gives the piece structure. Each arrival (except, of course, the last) is also a point of departure, so the music moves forward with what might be called a pogo stick effect. How the points of arrival affect the music's movement depends on how final, how clear, and how emphatic they are.

Finality of Arrival

Composers usually give their pieces clear and decisive conclusions.

Any symphony by Haydn, Mozart, or Beethoven makes its final arrival this way. But throughout a piece composers also distribute intermediate points of arrival that close off cycles of movement. Unlike final points of arrival, these leave the door open to further movement. In this sense, music closely parallels language. The varying degrees of finality in music are analogous to points of punctuation in language—commas, semicolons, periods, question marks, and exclamation points. A simple series of eight taps can illustrate the point. Since we tend to group taps by twos and fours we can assign a comma value to the fourth tap and a period value to the eighth tap.

EXAMPLE 4-2   Punctuation and arrival.

```
1     1     1    1,     1     1     1    1.
           comma                       period
```

Using the familiar terms of language, we can rate degrees of finality in musical arrival accordingly:

        least effect of finality = momentary breath, no punctuation
      partial effect of finality = comma, semicolon
    avoided effect of finality = question mark
      full effect of finality = period, exclamation point

The various degrees of finality can be used in different ways to reinforce the expressive qualities of a piece. Mozart, in his Sonata in A Major (Example 4-3), maintains exquisite balance among all the aspects of the piece—sound, movement, and arrival—by holding them in place with evenly spaced and properly graded points of "punctuation." Accordingly, the sonata's theme conveys an all's-right-with-the-world feeling. Haydn, on the other hand, packs the first few measures of his Sonata in E♭ Major with challenging contradictions (Example 4-4). He reaches four successive final-sounding points of arrival at the very outset of the piece. Yet not one of these halts the movement; they simply hold it back momentarily. Then, after using a bold downward swoop to head once more toward a decisive point of arrival, Haydn throws in what we hear as a combination exclamation point and question mark! In these examples Mozart expresses an elegant serenity while Haydn is full of biting wit that parodies a stately manner.

Both the Mozart and the Haydn examples come from the openings of movements, showing the effects of finality on a small scale. At the end of a long work, the composer generally escalates the effect of impending final arrival. He forges a chain of closing gestures to create an

* EXAMPLE 4-3   Mozart: Sonata in A Major, first movement.

* EXAMPLE 4-4   Haydn: Sonata in E♭ Major, first movement.

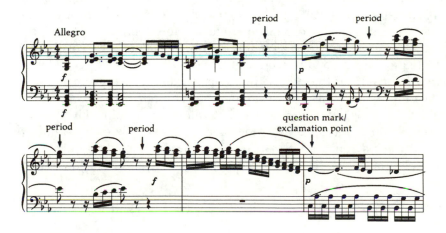

area of arrival. This is especially characteristic of nineteenth-century symphonic and operatic music. Beethoven fashions one of the most stirring windups of any major work at the very end of his Symphony no. 3. A rousing set of fanfares builds to a series of brilliant and emphatic strokes that recall the arresting start of the symphony.

Not all works end with such forceful finality. Brahms closes his Symphony no. 3 with a gradual evaporation of sound, so that even after the music has ceased, you remain in a spell of stillness. Schubert also leaves something unsettled at the end of his song "Die Stadt" ("The City").

The eerie mood he has conjured up by the ghostly vision of a dream city is prolonged by the totally restless effect with which he ends the song. Thus, the way a composer ends a piece can crystallize the ideas he has expressed throughout the work.

Clarity and Emphasis of Arrival

Arrival is clear when we sense a well-defined pause or break in musical movement. Most familiar songs have clear points of arrival for their various phrases. "The Star-Spangled Banner" starts with two:

"Oh, say can you *see*" (arrival)
"By the dawn's early *light*" (arrival)

Full clarity of arrival, if maintained throughout a composition and regularly spaced, will tend to make the music immediately intelligible. Songs and dances, such as Johann Strauss's *Blue Danube Waltz*, observe this procedure faithfully. Music that has a speculative, searching quality, however, will often mask its intermediate points of arrival. Bach was the master of this art. In the first fugue of *The Well-Tempered Clavier*, Book I, Bach deploys only two points of arrival—one midway through the piece, the other at its conclusion. Actually, the opening solo melody hints at a point of arrival as it rounds off, but then Bach covers the punctuation as a second part enters before the first finishes. He reduces clarity of arrival for the cumulative effect of continued movement.

A composer may also overstate intermediate arrivals. This tends to build a drive toward a later arrival that will be unquestionably clear at its proper time. Beethoven provides a striking example of this kind of tradeoff in his Sonata in E♭ Major, Example 4-5, below. He arranges three bold and very closely spaced points of arrival. Then, just when

* EXAMPLE 4-5   Clarity of arrival. Beethoven: Sonata in E♭ Major, second movement.

you may expect the fourth point as a continuation of this pattern, he masks that point and moves the music powerfully forward to reach a more decisive point later. The irregular treatment of arrival, the rich, low sound, and the slow pace combine to create the air of great portent indicated by Beethoven's tempo marking, which means "broadly, with great expression."

Varying the emphasis of arrival can entirely change what the music expresses. If, in the finger-tapping exercise, Example 4-2, you strike the last of the eight taps much more forcefully than you do the preceding taps, you convey a sense of firm intention, perhaps even a touch of violence. If, on the contrary, you strike the final tap much more lightly— deemphasizing the effect of arrival—you convey something entirely different: questioning, surprise, even indecision. Beethoven makes a wonderful play with these effects at the beginning of his Symphony no. 7 in A Major. The stroke that opens the piece and the intermediate points of arrival formed by the three subsequent strokes are emphatic. The next point of arrival, a few seconds later, is hushed. The contrast between the two kinds of arrival highlights the mercurial changes in feeling that Beethoven expresses here.

Approaching the Point of Arrival

The way music moves leads us to anticipate its points of arrival; conversely, those arrivals control and shape the musical movement. But consider your perceptions and feelings as movement *approaches* its point of arrival. In Example 4-3 above, the first movement of his Sonata in A Major, Mozart conveys a comfortable feeling. He delivers arrival exactly on schedule, as if the music were running by clockwork. This is a pleasant, reassuring experience, especially when the music has such elegant charm. Beethoven, on the other hand, conveys in his Sonata in E♭ Major (Example 4-5 above) a feeling of suspense, of being caught up short, by repeatedly interrupting the movement with emphatic yet only intermediate points of arrival.

In the first two or three minutes of his Symphony no. 3, Beethoven demonstrates the compelling effect of arrival delayed. He drives the movement forward, using ingenious tactics to prolong the drive: he promises—then withholds—the effect of closure by sudden interruptions, by spinning out movement, by undermining effects of finality. Each decisive point of arrival along the way is at the same time a point of departure for the next broad cycle of movement. The very power of the drive followed by the hammering effect of arrival provides springboards for further action—as if arrival were inadequate, except at the end, to hold movement in check.

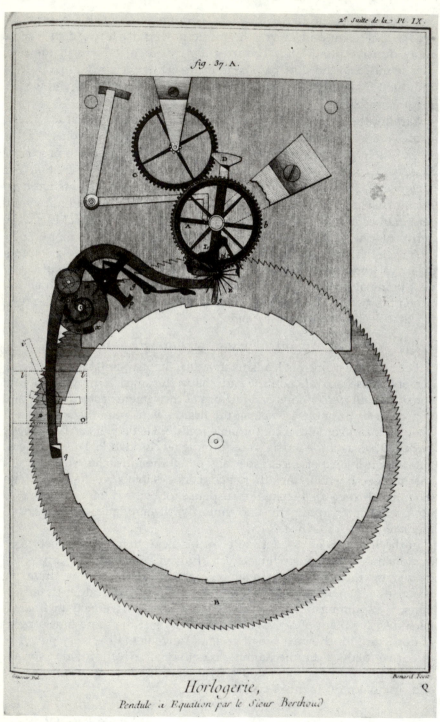

fig. 37. A.

Horlogerie,
Pendule à Equation par le Sieur Berthoud

Horlogerie (Watchmaking).

5

The Process of Rhythm

WE NOW SHIFT OUR FOCUS. In the first four chapters, our responses as listeners were the center of attention. We explored ways in which effects of sound, movement, and arrival touch our musical sensibilities, how they stir our feelings. Now we enter the composer's workshop to get a look at some of the musical processes by which composers create these effects. They include the basic elements and processes of music—rhythm, melody, harmony, and texture.

Rhythm measures and manages musical time. It measures time by note values and by meter. It manages time by arranging various patterns of note values in order to give character to a passage. Example 5-1 demonstrates the difference between simple measurement and expressive management of musical time. To get a feel for the difference, tap out the series of equal taps in 5-1a at a rate of one per second. It becomes monotonous and meaningless very quickly. Now, divide each alternate tap into two shorter ones, as in 5-1b. You immediately set up a character, an attitude; as you continue, this pattern tends to assert itself and convey a simple and well-defined message, a sort of musical Morse code.

EXAMPLE 5-1   Measurement and management of rhythm.

a. Measurement: 1 1 1 1 1 1 1 1 1 1 1 1 . . . etc.
b. Management: 1 111 111 111 111 111 1

Note values and meter are explained in the Appendix, "How to Read Music." Here we deal with rhythm as a process, focusing on the way it imparts character and expression to musical sounds.

Duple and Triple Time

The very heart of the rhythmic process lies in the distinction between duple time (1-2, 1-2, 1-2) and triple time (1-2-3, 1-2-3, 1-2-3). When a composer decides to use either duple or triple time he commits himself to one basic kind of motion. For example, Johann Strauss Jr. used the swinging triple meter of a waltz rhythm to give his *Blue Danube Waltz* its unique lilt; John Philip Sousa took a rapid duple beat to give his "Stars and Stripes Forever" march its crisp, authoritative air.

Suppose we take a series of seven beats and organize them, first in duple meter, then in triple meter:

EXAMPLE 5-2   Duple and triple meters.

Duple: 1̲ – 2   1̲ – 2   1̲ – 2   1̲
Triple: 1̲ – 2 – 3   1̲ – 2 – 3   1̲

In each of these series, the beats marked 1̲ represent departure and arrival, while the others represent movement. Duple meter hits the ground more often than triple meter. Conversely, triple meter moves along further in each of its units, and has fewer points of arrival. The underlined notes are accented; they receive stress and are called downbeats. The notes between those underlined are unaccented; they lack stress and are called upbeats. The alternation of accented and unaccented notes is an essential feature of musical rhythm.

Rhythmic Patterns

When you feel that the mood of a piece is "jazzy," "stately," "like a march," "waltz-like," or reminiscent of some other kind of dance, you are responding to something very basic in the form and content of the piece. You are responding to rhythmic patterns that have a distinct personality.

When you tapped out the long and short notes of Example 5-1b you were creating rhythmic patterns—short, coherent groupings of notes of different lengths. In compositions, such patterns are signals; they suggest expressive qualities that you respond to. Rhythmic patterns are countless. They range from the simplest two-note groups, as in the first strain of *The Blue Danube Waltz*, to highly complex combinations, as in the introduction and opening strain of "The Stars and Stripes Forever." For most listeners, the most familiar rhythmic patterns are those heard in traditional and popular dances. Each dance has its own pattern, by which we recognize the dance and respond to its expressive message. Example 5-3 illustrates rhythmic patterns typical of marches (duple time) and minuets (triple time).

EXAMPLE 5-3

a. Typical march rhythm

b. Typical minuet rhythm

Other dances in duple time (most of them originating in folklore) include the gavotte (see Example 10-6), bourrée (see Example 11-3), habanera, polka, schottische, reel, czardas, galop, contredanse, fox trot, tango, and ragtime. Other dances in triple time include the sarabande (see Example 4-5), polonaise, gigue, mazurka, furiant, courante, hornpipe, passepied, and Swabian allemande.

The contribution of dance to music goes far beyond the obvious and recognizable appearance of a particular dance rhythm in a piece. Composers in all genres—concert, theater, and church music—have drawn from the dance. Much of their early training as well as their mature professional work includes dance composition. They have taken the rhythmic patterns, absorbed the qualities of movement that characterize various dances, and trimmed musical action to the balances and symmetries of dance. Beethoven began the principal theme of the first movement of his Symphony no. 3 with a waltz tune. Mozart opened his *Jupiter* Symphony in the mood of a grand march, later to touch upon

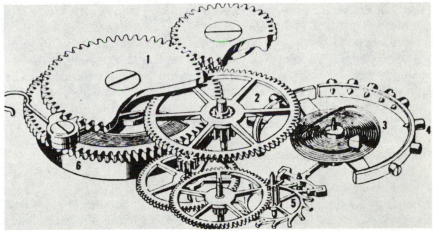

The gears of a modern watch.

gavotte and sarabande rhythms. Bach chose a polonaise rhythm to spark the mood of exultation in the "Et Resurrexit" of his Mass in B Minor. Mendelssohn used both tarantella and saltarello patterns for local color in his *Italian* Symphony. Richard Strauss used an eccentric gigue in *Till Eulenspiegel* as a musical signal of mischief for the comic hero who plays tricks on everyone.

Even though note values are established by a mechanical method of division and multiplication, they have an important effect on musical expression. It may be difficult, even impossible, for a listener to detect a difference in movement between $\frac{3}{4}$ and $\frac{3}{8}$ time, but for composers and performers, dealing with eighth notes will tend to produce a somewhat lighter, more buoyant effect than if the same music were written in quarter notes. Actually, in the eighteenth century many musicians felt that certain meters were suited for certain kinds of expression. Indeed, the meters and expressive qualities of some compositions do match:

$\frac{3}{2}$ the half note is the triple-time unit underpinning the deliberate, broadly swinging "Crucifixus" from the Mass in B Minor by Bach

$\frac{4}{4}$ the quarter note is the unit in brisk duple time that frames Figaro's humorous "Non piu andrai" in *The Marriage of Figaro* by Mozart

$\frac{3}{4}$ a relatively quick movement of quarter notes grouped by threes gives considerable buoyancy and drive to the first movement of Beethoven's Symphony no. 3

$\frac{6}{8}$ a quick, driving rhythm in eighth notes, strongly suggestive of the hectic frenzy of the "Witches' Sabbath," is heard in the finale of Berlioz's *Symphonie Fantastique*

Meter and expression match often enough to consider the connection valid, but the music's color and feeling depend just as much on tempo, rhythmic pattern, and how the performers play the piece.

Since tempo instructions from composer to performer are often vague, different performers interpret them differently. Hence, you may find one orchestra's reading of a symphony as much as five minutes longer than another's. For you as a listener, the only criterion for preference will be to determine which reading presents the content of the music most clearly. Does the pace seem to drag? Is it too slow to maintain buoyancy in the action? Or is it too hasty, making it difficult for you to follow the sense of the music?

Rhythm in Musical Form

We have explored rhythmic processes—duple and triple time and rhythmic patterns—in terms of brief time frames, often a matter of seconds. But we also feel rhythm at work on a large scale when, for example, the music changes manner from one section to another, or when it rises to a peak, or when it reaches an emphatic point of arrival. This kind of rhythm is analogous to the grand rhythms in our lives—waking/sleeping, day/night, working/resting, even the tide of the seasons. For example, we can grasp a rhythm in the very clear shifts in attitude through the various strains of "The Stars and Stripes Forever." Sousa first catches our attention with a rousing, brief introduction. Next he gives us a light, catchy first strain and a bold, much heavier second strain. He then introduces the singing tune we all associate with this march. An agitated interlude then prepares us for a second hearing of the tune. The grand rhythm of this piece thus plays strains of relatively equal length against each other in a contrast of heavy and light action. We shall observe other aspects of long-range rhythm when we deal specifically with musical form in chapters 10 and 11.

The Flute by Felix Valloton, 1896, woodcut, 12¼" × 9⅞". Collection, The Museum of Modern Art, New York. Gift of Victor S. Riesenfeld.

6

The Process of Melody

MELODY IS THE MOST TANGIBLE ELEMENT OF MUSIC, the most easily recognized and remembered. Think of the "Ode to Joy" from Beethoven's Symphony no. 9, the Beatles's "Yesterday," Franz Gruber's "Silent Night," "The Waltz of the Flowers" from Tchaikovsky's *Nutcracker* Suite. We cherish these tunes and so many others; they are among the most precious moments in the art of music.

The Contour of Melody

Basically, melody is a line of notes with a contour. It may rise or fall; it may remain on a level; it may be rounded or jagged; it may have a wide or narrow range. Each of these patterns contributes to musical meaning and expression. As the gestures of a dancer or actor convey a mood on the stage, or as the path of an artist's pencil gradually builds a meaningful image, so does a line of notes build a melodic shape. When a melodic line rises steadily, it can suggest increasing energy or tension; when it drops steadily, it can suggest relaxation or a sense of settling. A melody that is more or less level, or has a narrow range of pitch, may suggest steadiness and evenness.

Abrupt rise or fall—particularly between high and low pitches—indicates bold, vigorous, or perhaps strenuous movement, especially if the pace is quick. When the melodic notes are next to each other in pitch, the melodic movement is described as conjunct. When gaps in pitch occur between successive notes, the melodic movement is described as disjunct. Example 6-1 illustrates conjunct and disjunct lines. Note how the changes in direction, the rise and fall, tend to compensate for each other. Such motion contributes to the sense of balance in the melody, in addition to its primary role in creating the melodic contour.

EXAMPLE 6-1 Melodic Shapes.

a. Connected or conjunct. Beethoven: Symphony no. 9, "Ode to Joy".

b. Disconnected or disjunct. Bach: Concerto for Two Violins in D Minor, first movement.

As a melody continues, it may arrive at an apex. This is a moment of high expressive intensity. In the beautifully lyric song by the Beatles, "Yesterday," the melody rises to an expressive apex on the words "all my troubles seemed *so far* away." The composer can shape an entire composition to rise to a grand melodic apex that gives a large-scale contour to the form of the piece. Wagner does so in his Prelude to *Tristan and Isolde,* and Bach does so in the second fugue of *The Well-Tempered Clavier,* Book I, in C Minor. Beethoven's Fifth Symphony shows how a melody can build to an expressive climax through a series of constantly higher apices (Example 6-2).

EXAMPLE 6-2 Melodic apices. Beethoven: Symphony no. 5, Op. 67.

Melodic Motives

Melodic contour joins with rhythmic patterns to create melodic figures or motives. For example, the most famous melodic motive in music, the opening of Beethoven's Fifth Symphony, has a rhythmic pattern of three short notes and one long note, and a melodic contour that drops downward by a short leap (Example 6-3):

EXAMPLE 6-3   Formation of a motive. Beethoven: Symphony no. 5, second movement.

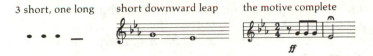

3 short, one long   short downward leap   the motive complete

Like gestures of one's hand, head, or body, a melodic motive can be very short yet convey a world of meaning. Whatever connotations this musical gesture may have carried for Beethoven himself, for us it has come to symbolize fate and, in the mid-twentieth century, victory in World War II. Given its bold, arresting motion, no one can question its aptness for these associations.

Melodic motives are the most easily recognized elements of musical form. Once you hear a motive, you can recognize it again later in the piece, and this helps you keep your bearings. A composer may repeat a motive exactly or vary it in many ways while retaining its similarity to what was heard before. He can introduce contrast among motives for the sake of variety or to create a kind of melodic tug-of-war that can intensify the ongoing action. Example 6-4 is concerned with repetition and variation: Beethoven states the four-note "fate" motive, repeats it at lower pitch, then restates it eleven times in varied forms to build

* EXAMPLE 6-4   Repetition and variation of motives. Beethoven: Symphony no. 5, first movement.

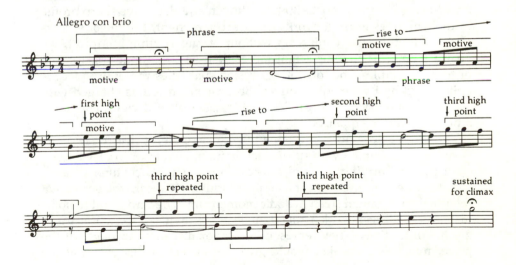

steadily upward to a point of climax. He uses the one figure exclusively here to spearhead the direction of the larger melodic line.

Mozart sets up a contrast between the motives in the next example (6-5). The whole orchestra begins with a flourish of three bold strokes; this is followed immediately by a reply which offers, in contrast, the merest fragment of a soft lyric melody. By going back and forth between "vigorous" and "singing" twice, Mozart sets in motion a rush of powerful musical action that pulls to a halt only fifteen measures later. Contrast here is a springboard for an exciting flight.

EXAMPLE 6-5   Contrast of motives. Mozart: Jupiter Symphony, beginning.

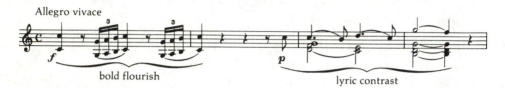

As you listen for melodic motives in any piece, note the number and variety of motives the composer uses. For example, to infuse the first movement of his Symphony no. 3 with its richness of content and breadth of form, Beethoven uses many different motives, which often stand in bold contrast to each other. In other works the composer may deal with just a few motives, constantly putting them into different situations and relationships. This was Bach's intention in the first movement of his *Brandenburg* Concerto no. 2. Both Beethoven and Bach give sharp profile to their motives in these works. In Gregorian chant, the melody flows along smoothly and conjunctly without strong rhythmic imprint; we hear a stream of melodic action rather than separate motives. In each of these examples, the idea of expression that rules the entire piece is epitomized by its melodic motives. Beethoven's music is charged with tremendous tension and conflict; Bach's has a playful vigor; chant has a floating, remote quality.

The motive does not represent a fully developed musical idea, yet its very brevity, coupled with its distinct manner, enables it to play a powerful role in carrying forward musical movement. Each time you encounter a new motive or hear a familiar motive reappear, you sense that the music has gained fresh melodic momentum. The important melodic materials of larger works, called subjects or themes, are made up of groups of motives. They represent topics for discourse throughout the piece, much as a speaker would give the subject of discussion at the beginning of a speech or debate and then refer to it throughout the presentation. Such themes are very tuneful and we enjoy them when they appear and reappear in their respective pieces. But their most important value to the music is the way they fit into the larger design of the work, both expressively and formally. Much music of the twentieth century absorbs melody into other processes—tone color, rhythm, harmony—so that we do not hear a continuous line of melodic action; rather, melody plays a role somewhat subordinate to those other processes, as in sections of Stravinsky's *Le Sacre du Printemps*.

Arrangements of Melodic Material

The simplest thing a composer can do with a tune is to repeat it. Popular and folk songs repeat one melody for all stanzas of a text. Folk dances also repeat tunes in this manner. Schubert, in his short but brilliant song "Ungeduld" ("Impatience"), uses one melody for all six stanzas. Each time, the tune rises to an impassioned climax to reiterate the urgent message of impatience.

The most common and useful way to treat melody in large-scale composition is to recall the theme, literally or varied. This is a principle in the form called rondo, where the opening theme, the refrain, returns after some intervening action like the chorus of a song. A rondo refrain has to be striking so that the listener can recognize it easily when it reappears. Mozart closes many of his piano concertos with rondo finales.

Recall can serve much the same purpose in music that rhyme serves in poetry—to match the sounds at the ends of a pair of lines *while changing the meaning*. We can call this procedure musical rhyme. Composers throughout the eighteenth and nineteenth centuries used it in large-scale works to create an overall melodic unity. For example, in his Sonata in F Major, Mozart closes an important musical segment about a third of the way through the first movement with the passage quoted in Example 6-6a; he then rhymes this passage *at a different level of pitch* to close the movement (Example 6-6b). Even if you do not read music, you can tell that the shapes are literally transposed. Such musical rhymes give you a clear sense of the unity of the piece. When music is linked to drama or poetry, melodic figures and themes can be used as musical "calling cards." Richard Wagner carries this process to its ultimate point, tagging persons, ideas, and situations with characteristic motives called "leitmotifs," by which you could recognize them. He makes striking use of this process in *Tristan and Isolde* to give two different nuances to the same basic idea. The tension and yearning that pervade the work are epitomized by the upward leap of the opening motive (Example 6-7). At the end of the opera Wagner recalls that motive, thereby creating a huge arch of meaning across four hours of music and drama. He makes,

EXAMPLE 6-6   Melodic rhyme. Mozart, Sonata in F Major, first movement.

a. End of first principal section

b. End of movement

however, a subtle but all-important change. Whereas the opening figure seems to trail off, the closing figure (Example 12-11c), continues on for two additional notes, C♯ and D♯, to give the line a strong and sustained effect of arrival.

If you have ever played an instrument or sung, you have probably felt the urge to embellish a given tune with a few touches of your own. Jazz, blues, and rock performers do that constantly. But it is not a new phenomenon. The tendency of performers to embellish melodies has been a powerful force in the evolution of musical styles throughout history. More formally, composers also embellish melodies, as part of the process of variation. The composer selects a melody, then writes a series of short pieces based on the shape of the melody, with various local changes to give each piece its own mood. The result is called a set

EXAMPLE 6-7   Beginning of Prelude to Tristan and Isolde.

of variations. Mozart uses the technique in his Sonata in A Major, Example 6-8a. In the first variation he decorates the melody with a whole cluster of piquant short notes (Example 6-8b), thus changing the quality of movement.

* EXAMPLE 6-8   Theme and variation. Mozart: Sonata in A Major, first movement. (On soundsheet as Example 4-3).

Melody can retain its identity while undergoing remarkable changes. One process of this sort is called development. The composer may change the melody's character, break it up into fragments to form new configurations, shift its range, vary its tone color. These are all techniques of development. Another and more spectacular way a composer may alter a melody is to transform it. If a melodic motive is clearly recognizable, the composer can set it in different expressive stances, different motions, different "costumes" without sacrificing its identity. Example 6-9 shows how Liszt transformed themes in his great Sonata in B Minor. He makes each transformation a new scene in a tableau of provocative poses, the musical counterpart of a Romantic melodrama. To make cer-

EXAMPLE 6-9   Thematic transformation. Liszt: Sonata in B Minor.

a. Theme I—brooding, introspective: descending line

Transformation—brilliant passage work

b. Theme II—bold, impassioned, electrifying: angular contour

Transformation—lyric, fanciful

c. Theme III—active, percussive: repeated tones

Transformation—songlike

tain that his hearer will recognize his themes despite their transformations, Liszt gives each theme a striking profile. Theme I moves steadily downward by step; theme II has an angular contour; theme III has a group of repeated notes caught up short by a twist at the end.

Meredith Willson provides another example of thematic transformation in his Broadway musical *The Music Man*. He uses the same basic tune for the framework of the sweetly sentimental waltz in triple time, "Good Night," and for the quick march in duple time, "Seventy-Six Trombones."

In this chapter we have looked at melody in many contexts—as motive, as tune, as theme, in development, in transformation, in embellishment and variation. For most of the music with which we are familiar, melody is the star actor taking center stage. But as the following chapters show, harmony shapes and directs the scene, rhythm propels it, and texture gives it color.

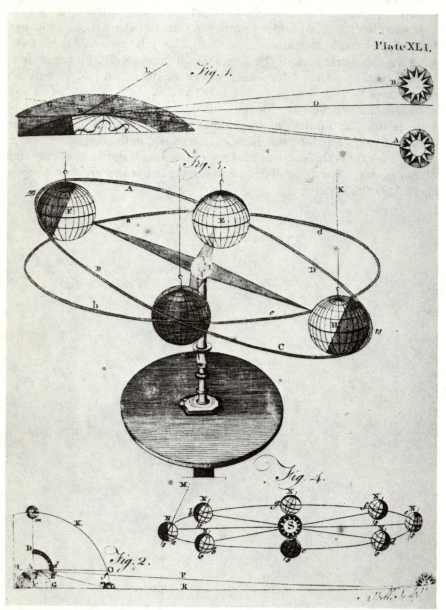

Eighteenth-century astronomy model.

7

The Process of Harmony

HARMONY IS CONCERNED WITH effects that are produced when two or more notes are sounded together. It also deals with the ways in which such effects can be used to promote musical movement and arrival. In chapter 2 we explored harmonic sound as color. Here we look at how harmony works in the movement–arrival cycle.

Stability, Instability

Sounds that are harmonically stable convey an impression of firmness, solidity, and restfulness. They serve as points of harmonic arrival. Sounds that are harmonically unstable convey an impression of imbalance and restlessness. They urge the music forward. Between the extremes of total stability and utter instability there are gradations, some of which are illustrated in Example 7-1. Generally speaking, stable com-

* EXAMPLE 7-1   Stability of harmonic sounds.

a. Very stable

b. Relatively stable

c. Relatively unstable

d. Highly unstable

binations are described as consonant while unstable combinations are dissonant.

Traditional Western harmony has established certain conventional progressions from unstable intervals to stable ones (any combination of two notes is called a harmonic interval). In Example 7-2, we hear the first interval as unstable, demanding some kind of resolution. The most satisfying resolution of that tension is to proceed to the second interval, which is stable. As such, it counteracts the edginess of the first interval with a mellow, sweet effect.

* EXAMPLE 7-2   Instability resolved by stability.

movement → arrival

Virtually every piece of music written from the eighteenth century to the beginning of the twentieth century uses this kind of harmonic progression extensively. A chain of such progressions can support the harmonic action of an entire piece. Example 7-3 shows a chain of these progressions in a simple context.

* EXAMPLE 7-3   Harmonic chain of progressions. (Up arrows designate instability; down arrows represent stability/arrival.)

This is the harmonic language with which concertgoers are most familiar. It is the language upon which both the simplest popular songs and the most profound symphonies draw. Schubert's well-known song, "Der Lindenbaum" ("The Linden Tree," Example 7-4) illustrates this meshing of processes. The points of stability are marked with down arrows, instability with up arrows; the cycles themselves with brackets. Notice Schubert's graceful wavelike melody that eventually rises to an expressive climax. He balances the sections both by making them the

EXAMPLE 7-4   Rhythm, melody, harmony combined. Schubert: "Der Lindenbaum" ("The Linden Tree").

same length and by repeating melodic material. Notice also how slowly he changes between stable and unstable harmonies.

Tonal Center, Key

When notes are sounded together, whether simultaneously or in succession, there seems to be a tendency for one note to assert itself in our hearing more strongly than others and thereby establish itself as a point of reference. You can illustrate this simply by humming a familiar song such as "My Old Kentucky Home" or "America." Stop humming just before the last note. The song is halted short of its goal. No matter what you do rhythmically or melodically, the sense of arrival necessary to round off the piece is missing *unless you hum that last note.* The last note (or tone) is a point of reference for the whole piece: it has established itself as a "tonal center." The Schubert song clearly centers on the note E. We hear it as a point of arrival in the melody in measures 6, 10, and 16. E is the tonal center for the piece, so we say that the piece is "in the key of E."

In traditional harmony, a key is a group of notes arranged around a central note, making use of progressions from instability to stability in order to direct the harmony toward that central note. Example 7-3 constantly hovers around the note C, touching it again and again to create an absolutely clear and firm effect of C as the point of harmonic reference, the "tonic."

Harmonic relationships are not the only way to establish a tonal center. A note begins to impress itself upon our attention also when it appears frequently and prominently in a passage. Medieval music and non-Western music locate their tonal centers this way, as in Example 7-5a. To show the subtle yet all-important difference between prominence and the interplay of stable and unstable sounds, a somewhat similar melody is given in Example 7-5b. This second melody uses the notes bracketed to create an instability–stability effect that ties a knot around the note C, securing its identity as the tonal center.

* EXAMPLE 7-5   Definition of tonal center.

a. By prominence

b. By interval relationship

Examples 7-5a and 7-5b each use much the same set of notes, but they define their respective keys in quite different ways. Notice the expressive effects these two methods project. Example 7-5a seems to float with a somewhat questioning effect while Example 7-5b asserts itself strongly.

If we take all the notes used in Example 7-5b and line them upward by steps, starting with the tonal center, C, we have the familiar major scale (do-re-mi-fa-so-la-ti-do), illustrated in Example 7-6a. It also shows the size of the steps from one note to the next in the major scale. Example 7-6b shows the steps in the minor scale. The most important difference between the major scale and the minor scale is the third note. The third note in the minor scale is lower by one half step than the third note in the major scale. This lowered third imparts to the minor key its dark, somewhat pathetic effect.

* EXAMPLE 7-6   Scales.

a. Major scale

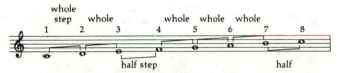

b. minor scale

Major and minor keys can set each other off very effectively. Beethoven took advantage of this contrast at the beginning of the fourth movement, the finale, of his Symphony no. 5. Toward the end of the third movement, the music is in a minor key, dark and brooding; then it builds quickly to burst into a massive, brilliant major sound to begin the finale. The minor key provides dramatic staging for the entry of the major.

Modulation: Change of Tonal Center

Modulation is the process of changing the tonal center. In Example 7-7a, for instance, the tonal center is clearly the note C. The tonal center changes in Example 7-7b when the note F♯ appears, leading to the note G as the new tonal center. In Example 7-7c, *after* the arrival at G, F♯ is replaced by F, and the tonal center shifts back to C.

In the Christmas carol "Adeste Fideles" ("O Come All Ye Faithful"), the music arrives at a new tonal center on "Come ye, o come ye to *Bethlehem*." It returns to the original tonal center, the home key, at the refrain "O come, let us adore him" and remains there for the rest of the song.

Eighteenth- and most nineteenth-century composers accepted as a basic requirement the idea that a movement should begin and end in the same key. Modulation is a technique they used to meet this basic requirement. Modulation raises a question by moving away from the

* EXAMPLE 7-7 Shifts of tonal center (modulation).

a. Tonal center remains on C

b. Tonal center shifts to G

c. Tonal center shifts to G, then back to C

home key. This question is answered by a compensating return to the home key. Meanwhile, the composer has created a bolder harmonic profile. In Example 7-7a above, the harmonic contour is flat, since the harmony remains in the home key, C:

C ——————————— C

In Example 7-7c the harmonic path has a marked profile due to the modulation to G:

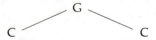

Modulation can involve a subtle shift of key, such as from C to its companion, G. It can also create a bold, colorful effect when the keys seem to lie musically "far apart." Beethoven, in the second movement of his Symphony no. 5, makes a surprising change of key after his opening songlike melody has run its course. He brings in a passage of total harmonic instability; we do not know where he is leading the music. Suddenly a brilliant melody in a new key bursts forth. Beethoven here combines all elements to create a blockbuster effect. He shifts the key color from soft and mellow to bright and dazzling, changes the motion from connected to detached, and transfers the orchestral sound from low strings to high brass. Beethoven liked this effect so much that he recalled it twice more in the course of the movement, each time setting it up with careful and deliberate shifts in harmonic color. Example 7-8 illustrates the first of these critical harmonic shifts.

sudden, brilliant
projection of new
strong sense of A♭   elements of instability introduced   and unexpected key: C

Chords

We have explored some of the basic processes of harmony—the stability–instability connection, tonal center, modulation—using chiefly
simple pairs of notes sounding together and single line examples. These
draw for us the threads that bind harmonic action. But harmony usually
deals with fuller sounds—chords. A chord consists of three or more
notes sounded at the same time. In traditional harmony, the basic chord
is called a triad, meaning a group of three. Composers have traditionally
used four types of triad, which differ according to the intervals between
their member notes. Example 7-9 illustrates these four types: major,
minor, augmented, and diminished. Each kind of triad has its own
characteristic sound. The major triad is bright and stable; the minor triad
is rather darker, yet quite stable; the diminished triad has a tight, dissonant quality, rather edgy; and the augmented triad has a rich, sweet
yet unstable effect.

* EXAMPLE 7-9   Formation of triads.

major minor major   minor major minor   minor minor dim.   major major aug.
third third triad   third third triad   third third triad   third third triad

The sweet sound of a song like "America the Beautiful" is based on
the many major triads it uses, while the darkness of the second movement, the funeral march, of Beethoven's Symphony no. 3 is due largely
to its minor triads. Diminished triads frequently appear at points of
instability in eighteenth- and nineteenth-century music. Augmented
triads, with their special color, appear much less frequently; Franz Liszt
had a particular liking for the augmented triad and gave it prominence

at the beginning of his *Faust Symphony* to suggest the restless introspection of the philosopher, Faust. If we place an additional note above
each of these triads at the interval of a seventh from the bottom note
(for example, C-E-G-B or G-B-D-F), the chord becomes a "seventh" chord
and takes on dissonance. (See the Appendix, "How to Read Music," for
more information on intervals.) Beethoven, showing his characteristic
boldness, began his Symphony no. 1 with an arresting dissonance, a
seventh chord.

Chords give body to the essential processes of harmony. They secure
stability; they intensify instability; they clarify and confirm keys; they
give color and force to modulation. They can accomplish these effects
because, like individual notes, they have relationships among each other.
To demonstrate this point, we look at how one key, C major, deploys
its triads.

Each note of a key—in this case C major—has a triad built upon it.
Example 7-10 illustrates these triads, showing the conventional desig-
nation of each triad by the Roman numeral and the name that describe
its position in the scale.

EXAMPLE 7-10   Triads in a major key.

| I | II | III | IV | V | VI | VII | I |
| tonic | supertonic | mediant | subdominant | dominant | submediant | leading tone | tonic |

For any given key, the triads I, IV, and V (and the seventh chord on
V) play the most important roles in shaping its harmonic progressions.
In the song "Silent Night," for instance, the sequence of chords is:

Silent night . . . All is calm, All is bright.
I   V   I
Round yon . . . mother . . . Holy Infant . . . tender . . .
IV   I   IV   I
Sleep . . . peace . . . heavenly . . . peace.
V   I   V   I

This progression gives a very clear impression of the major key.

Cadences

In "Silent Night," pauses in the motion were regularly spaced. Some
were strongly marked, some lightly marked in their effect of punctuat-

ing the line. A progression of chords leading immediately to a strong or light pause is called a cadence. Example 7-11 shows how different kinds of cadence in a passage in C major work within the key to indicate and confirm it.

* EXAMPLE 7-11   Cadences.

A. The progression marked A is a *half* cadence; it makes a pause or break in the musical action comparable to what a comma or semicolon makes in a sentence. It consists of a stop on V.
B. The progression marked B is a *deceptive* cadence; it "deceives" the ear by substituting some other chord for the I chord the ear expects following a V chord. Usually, the substitute chord is a VI.
C. The progression marked C is an *authentic* cadence; it provides a final effect of harmonic arrival, a solid and square embodiment of the home key. In its simplest form it consists of V moving to I, usually with the roots of the two harmonies—G and C, respectively, in this case—assigned to the bass. An authentic cadence is comparable to a period in language: each completes a line of action or thought.
D. The progression marked D is a *plagal* cadence; it moves from IV to I. We are familiar with this progression as the "amen" of a hymn. It often follows an authentic cadence as a means to settle the harmony, something like an afterthought.

This chapter has described the traditional Western system of harmony, which was in force for at least three centuries. Although many twentieth-century composers have gone beyond the traditional system to explore tonal relationships that had not previously been usable, their early training in the standard harmonic language gave them a firm footing that served them well in their explorations. Moreover, a great deal of the musical talent of our age is involved with popular, theatrical, and broadcast music, all of which relies heavily upon the cadences and keys of the traditional harmonic system.

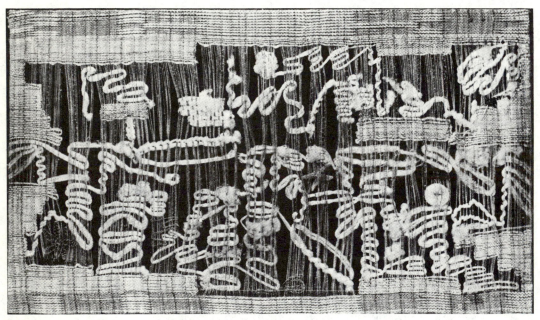

Wall Hanging with Sea-Stars by Else Regensteiner.

8

The Process of Texture

THE FULL SOUND OF A COMPOSITION, as you hear it, is built from individual lines. We designate these lines as voices or parts regardless whether they are played by instruments or sung. Each voice or part is assigned its particular kind of action, as though it were one dancer or actor among an ensemble. Their composite action, the total effect of their sound and motion, constitutes musical texture. For example, a string quartet produces one texture when each instrument is busy spinning out its own flurry of short notes, and produces a different texture when three instruments play long notes together to accompany a soloist. You would hear yet another texture if exactly the same music were played by a brass quartet.

The principal textural roles a voice might be assigned are:

1. a principal melody
2. a supporting bass line
3. a middle part, less prominent, that fills in the sound
4. a melodic line working against another melodic line
5. a line moving in the same pattern as the principal melody, but at a different pitch

The textures created by these roles are of two general types: (1) homophonic, in which a single principal melodic idea is presented, and (2) polyphonic, or contrapuntal, in which two or more important melodic lines are heard at the same time.

Homophonic Texture

Simple melody and accompaniment, such as singing to plucked guitar sounds, represents the most familiar and accessible kind of texture. From the earliest moments of our musical history to the present day, this kind of melody–accompaniment texture has been front and center in music-making. Accompaniments use various patterns—struck chords, sustained tones, or a pattern of light, quickly moving notes as in Example 8-1, where the simple accompaniment figure creates a light and flowing sense of movement.

EXAMPLE 8-1   Melody and accompaniment texture. Mozart: Sonata in C Major, second movement.

The next Example (8-2) is also homophonic, since the heavy chords support a powerful melody in the uppermost voice. But notice that all voices are moving in the same rhythmic pattern, to reinforce the melody, rather than set it off. This kind of texture is called chordal.

* EXAMPLE 8-2   Chordal texture. Beethoven: Symphony no. 5, last movement. (On soundsheet as Example 2-3)

Polyphonic Texture

When a single voice performs a melody without accompaniment, the texture is designated as monophonic, meaning "one-voiced." When two or more voices perform the same melodic line, the texture is designated as unison. When several voices play clearly separate lines, each with some degree of melodic importance, the texture is called polyphonic (meaning "many-voiced") or contrapuntal.

The simplest kind of polyphonic texture is created by imitation. In imitation, one part begins with a melody; very shortly a second part enters with the same melody, while the first continues to spin out its line. Imitation may involve as few as two parts or as many as five or six separate parts. A familiar type of imitative polyphony is the round, such as "Row, Row, Row Your Boat." In singing such a piece, you feel your part working against the others in a neatly fitted texture. Imitation can also be used to build a tight, continuous line of action in broadly scaled, complex pieces. Example 8-3 illustrates this procedure in a prelude by Bach; note the sense of drive and accumulation he builds as the voices enter successively.

* EXAMPLE 8-3   Imitative polyphonic texture. Bach: Prelude in E♭ Major, The Well-Tempered Clavier, Book 1.

Counterpoint *without* imitation fits two or more different melodies to each other. One of the most delightful examples of this is the final strain of Sousa's "The Stars and Stripes Forever." The trombones give us the wonderful tune in their full-throated middle register while the piccolos dance in the stratosphere with their sprightly jumping figures—a marvelous counterpoint of color, register, rhythm, and conjunct versus disjunct melody. In a more serious vein, the three lines at the beginning of Brahms's Symphony no. 1—rising, falling, and level—embody this nonimitative kind of counterpoint, called free counterpoint.

Homophonic texture lends itself to clear pauses and regular movement, governed by the leading voice. In polyphonic texture, the overlapping of voices disguises pauses and therefore promotes a continuous flow. Composers often use elements of homophonic and polyphonic texture together or side by side. For example, Brahms opens his Symphony no. 1 with two important melodic lines in the upper voices, one descending, the other rising. Underneath, the steady beat of the accompanying bass repeats the same note; it adds a firm homophonic-style support to the upper voices. Also, while there are but three important

Landscape, Giorgio Morandi, 1933, 8¹⁄₁₆″ × 11¹³⁄₁₆″. Collection, The Museum of Modern Art, New York. Given anonymously.

melodic lines, the entire orchestra is deployed to reinforce these lines—
a procedure called doubling.

The principal melody can also be handed back and forth among performers or among various parts in a game of give-and-take. Jazz thrives
on give-and-take; Dixieland could not exist without it. The exchange
can be very clear, as in Dixieland, or it can be very subtle, as when an
accompaniment figure takes on momentary interest; it may even suggest
an imitation of the principal melody, as in Example 8-4.

EXAMPLE 8-4   Give-and-take texture. Beethoven: Sonata in B♭ Major,
second movement.

Adagio, con molta espressione

Beethoven, throughout the first movement of his Symphony no. 3,
weaves in a wide variety of textures. These reinforce the rich melodic
content, the striking rhythmic play, and the bold harmonic action of this
movement. Full chordal texture, simple melody–accompaniment, give-
and-take, imitation, free counterpoint, unisons, melody with elaborate
rhythmic accompaniment—these are some of the textures that Beethoven alternates, often rapidly, to contribute to the electrifying impact of
this piece.

One important aspect of texture is the way the actual sounds of the
various voices blend or contrast. For example, when a viola and cello
are playing together in counterpoint, they may sound more blended
than when, say, an oboe is playing a melody accompanied by a sustained trombone. Berlioz bases much of his contrapuntal writing upon
this principle. Again and again in his *Symphonie Fantastique* he sharpens
the contrapuntal effect by assigning lines to instruments of strikingly
different color. The opening of the fourth movement, "The March to
the Scaffold," is a particularly bold example of contrast in instrumental
tone color that sharpens the contrapuntal action.

Each conscientious performer or conductor makes a special study of
the textures in a piece. He must have a clear idea of the degree of blend
or separation. This is necessary so that the composer's idea comes through

clearly and undistorted. How often in a performance do we miss an important figure or voice because of a poorly projected texture—thereby losing for a time the thread of movement and the meaning of the music itself?

The two most important voices or parts in a musical texture have traditionally been the outer, that is, the lowermost and uppermost, parts. This is simply because we can hear better what goes on in these parts than we can the inner parts. Outer voices form the skeleton of most musical textures, with other voices filling in for richer sound, as Example 8-5 illustrates:

EXAMPLE 8-5   Interplay of outer voices. Haydn: Quartet in D Major, first movement.

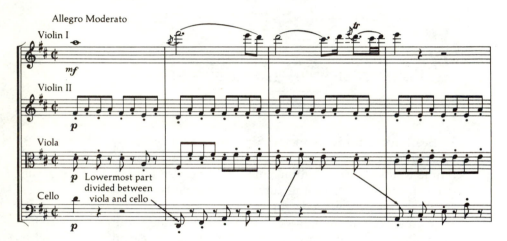

Texture is a telling indicator of historical styles. We can illustrate this point with two highly contrasted treatments of texture, each typical of its era: a Renaissance motet for voices and a modern work for a small group of instruments, Stravinsky's *L'Histoire du Soldat*.

Renaissance motet

1. Blend of voices; homogeneity of sound
2. Limited range of sound

L'Histoire du Soldat

1. Sharp contrast between voices; heterogeneity of sound
2. Wide range of sound; wide separation in instrumental pitches

3. Much contrapuntal activity but, because of points 1 and 2, not a strong impression of the independence of voices

3. Strong impression of contrapuntal activity, even when a melodic line is supported by accompaniment; this is due to the extreme independence of voices and their lack of blend

The palette of textures from which composers can choose is incredibly rich. Like melody, texture takes on vitality and color through the inventiveness of the composer.

Illustration for *The Wandering Jew* by Gustave Doré.

9

The Process of Association

ONE OF THE GREATEST APPEALS OF MUSIC is its ability to evoke moods and images. Composers in every age and of every rank—amateurs as well as the masters—have taken advantage of the evocative power of music to suggest associations with words, pictures, and gestures.

The range of this associative power is vast. The composer can project deep feeling over an entire piece, as Handel did in the jubilation of the "Hallelujah Chorus" from his *Messiah*. The composer can imitate a specific action, as Saint-Saëns did when he used swooping, sliding figures to pinpoint the braying of asses in his *Carnival of Animals*. You may find it helpful to think of musical associations as topics, subjects for presentation and discussion in a piece of music. In this way, topics serve much the same purpose in music as an idea or theme does in a literary presentation. They can be signals that direct your attention to specific points in the music or they can furnish material for the composer's discussion throughout a piece. Moreover, topics add color and interest to your listening experience. Knowing and recognizing them can bring you closer to the music and enhance your enjoyment of it.

Topics as Signals

Cue music—a short, characteristic, easily recognizable motive—is the most obvious kind of musical signal. The brilliance of the "Masterpiece Theater" theme, the excitement of the *William Tell* Overture fragment that introduced "The Lone Ranger," the short tunes that characterize the players in Prokofieff's *Peter and the Wolf*—these are striking, cleverly wrought musical signals to which we quickly respond. However brief signals may be, they set up certain expectations. They are attractive fragments, disembodied yet evocative.

Composers frequently incorporate signals into complete works. Bee-thoven heralded the rescue of the hero, Florestan, in his opera *Fidelio* with a bold trumpet call. The excitement of the hunt is graphically depicted by the imitation of dogs barking in fourteenth-century hunting songs. Haydn must have had a wonderful time writing pictorial effects in his great oratorio *The Creation*. The work abounds with tiny bits of description—mountains, rivers, birds, and beasts of all kinds.

Topics for Discussion

Dances

Throughout the centuries dances have been composers' most fruitful source for musical topics. Their distinctive patterns are easily recognized whenever they appear and their qualities of movement suggest moods or expressive attitudes. When we hear dance and march rhythms today, independently or in a larger work, we respond to their general manner, their pace, their rhythm, their sense of movement. But in the seventeenth and eighteenth centuries, people read these motions also as indications of dignity and social status. For example, the sarabande, the court minuet, the gavotte, and the pavane were identified with royal and aristocratic status. The bourrée, the quicker minuet, the gigue, the ballroom waltz, and others had middle-level status; while the contredanse, the Ländler, and the Swabian allemande were signs of the lower class.

Operagoers in the eighteenth century were familiar with these topics. When they heard a solemn march, they knew that a priest or king was about to take center stage. When they heard a simple tune in waltz time supported by a drone (a sustained note in the bass), they knew it introduced some low-born character, a servant or a peasant. Instrumental music took the cue from opera and imitated this characteristic use of topic, often with greater flexibility and humor.

Alla Breve

In addition to dances, many other topics found their way into concert and operatic music. Most of these came into prominence during the eighteenth century and were still used as part of the musical vocabulary of the nineteenth century. Of these topics, the one at the top of the scale of dignity was music identified with the church. In its purest form this music maintained a slow and deliberate pace, using mostly whole notes and half notes. For this reason, it was sometimes called the *alla breve*, meaning "in the manner of the breve" (whole note). Since it kept a steady, connected motion with no breaks or sharp turns it was also called the *stile legato*, the bound style. Any chorale or solemn hymn tune

Sarabande dancers.

draws upon this style, whether named so or not. Martin Luther used it for his well-known chorale, "A Mighty Fortress is our God." Mozart borrowed it and quickened its pace to begin the finale of his *Jupiter Symphony*. Bach used the *alla breve* style in a deeply tragic statement, the "Crucifixus" from his Mass in B Minor (which will be discussed in chapter 12).

Learned Style

In another topic ranking high in dignity, the learned style, the composer exercises his skill in counterpoint. We hear the learned style at its most dignified when the melodic material draws on the *alla breve* (as in Example 8-3, from the Bach Prelude in E♭ Major). However, it can also raise the dignity of other topics—dances, marches, even songlike melodies—by treating them contrapuntally, as in Example 9-1 from Beethoven's Symphony no. 3. The lower line is the symphony's familiar waltz theme; the upper line is a sprightly figure with a rhythm suggesting the polonaise. Alone, each is rather ordinary in effect. Together, they make a delightful and subtle bit of musical wit—a touch of the high style.

EXAMPLE 9-1   Popular topics (polonaise and waltz) in learned setting.
Beethoven: Symphony no. 3, first movement.

Ombra

Still another topic of serious import is the *ombra*. The term means "shadow" or "shade," and refers to supernatural manifestations: ghosts, spirits, gods, and devils. These are frequently introduced into serious theater, as in Shakespeare's *Hamlet,* where the ghost of Hamlet's father appears in the opening scene to set the whole wheel of action in motion. Generally, the sightlines of *ombra* are turned downward to Limbo and Hell. *Ombra* uses much the same techniques as the *alla breve*—slow, deliberate, regular motion—but it colors the action with instabilities, shifting harmonies, and chiaroscuro effects of scoring to project a mood of dread, chaos, even terror. Mozart paints an overwhelming air of supernatural retribution and doom in the climactic "supper scene" of *Don Giovanni* as he brings the statue of the murdered commandant on stage with magnificent, bone-chilling *ombra* music. Haydn depicts the shadowy vagueness of "Chaos" by beginning *The Creation* with elusive *ombra* sounds and figures. Beethoven evokes much the same mood at the beginning of his Symphony no. 4—and shortly thereafter builds a brilliant contrast with a buoyant dancelike tune.

Other Topics

The fanfare, lower on the scale of dignity, turns up very often in concert and theater music of the eighteenth and nineteenth centuries. These are trumpet, horn, and bugle calls, often played by the brass themselves or imitated by other instruments. Chopin's *Polonaise Militaire* has the fanfare as well as the drum rhythm of a military scene. Hunting calls also suggest a military/cavalier topic. Example 9-2 illustrates a typical hunting call pattern, one that Haydn uses with great variety and ingenuity as a prominent theme in the finale of his Symphony no. 103 in E♭ Major.

EXAMPLE 9-2   Hunting call figure.

Other topics of moderate dignity, the brilliant and the singing styles, generally aim to entertain the listener rather than to instruct or move deeply. The brilliant style shows off the performer's skill with rapid passages and glittering figuration. Any solo concerto has many such passages. Bach provides a beautiful illustration of several voices meshing in a clockwork of brilliant-style figures in Example 9-3. He gives each of the four voices its own rhythmic pattern—truly an exuberant exercise!

The singing style provides an effective foil to the brilliant style. In the singing style we hear lyrical, tuneful music suitable for vocal performance. The song "Drink To Me Only With Thine Eyes" represents the singing style par excellence. "Dido's Lament" from Purcell's opera *Dido and Aeneas* (Example 9-4) is a magnificent example of the singing style. In its deep, poignant pathos this lament brings the singing style to the highest level. Note how the poignancy of the broadly arched *alla breve* melody is intensified by dissonances that it forms with the bass.

EXAMPLE 9-3   Brilliant style. Bach: Brandenburg Concerto no. 2, first movement.

* EXAMPLE 9-4   Singing style. Purcell: Dido and Aeneas, "Dido's Lament."

Finally, we arrive at the lowest level on the scale of dignity: topics associated with low-born persons—shepherds, peasants, and servants. Music that depicts such characters is typically simple and tuneful, tends to repeat figures, has very little elaboration, and often is set to a quick patter in the text. At the beginning of Mozart's *Don Giovanni*, Leporello enters with a simple march tune that identifies his low station as Don Giovanni's servant.

The most characteristic music for low-born persons is the musette. In this style the bass holds a note for some time while a single upper voice intones a simple melody or a set of flourishes. Examples of the musette topic abound in music. Beethoven sets the pastoral mood of his Symphony no. 6 with a simple drone bass. Schubert's song "Der Leiermann"

Pl. VII.

Chapiteaux des cinq Ordres, avec le Chapiteau Ionique
Moderne.

Chapiteau Toscan.

Chapiteau Dorique.

Chapiteau Ionique.

Chapiteau Ionique Moderne.

Chapiteau Corinthien.

Chapiteau Composite.

2 Modules, ou 24 minutes.

2 Modules, ou 36 minutes.

Architecture.

Chapiteaux des cinq Ordres.

("The Hurdy-Gurdy Man," Example 9-5) derives its heartbreaking pathos from the reiterated drone and the fragment of plaintive melody that alternates with the short-breathed declamation of the singer.

* EXAMPLE 9-5   Low-style musette.   Schubert: "Der Leiermann" ("The Hurdy-Gurdy Man").

(Up be-hind the vil-lage stands an or-gan-man,)

In the present century, the drone–musette topic appears as a gentle bucolic effect in Arthur Honegger's *Pastoral d'Été*, and as a hectic preparation for a wild dance in the opening measures of the finale of Bartók's *Concerto for Orchestra*. Composers sometimes take the musette up into the higher styles as well. In the first movements of Mozart's Quintet in C Major, and in Beethoven's Quartet in F Major, Op. 59, no. 1, musette style contributes significantly to the breadth of gesture that marks these movements as among the greatest works of either composer.

Exotic Topics

To invoke colorful, exotic moods, various composers have drawn on Moorish and Chinese dances (Tchaikovsky, *Nutcracker* Suite), Scottish melodic style (Mendelssohn, *Scotch* Symphony), Spanish flamenco (Rimsky-Korsakoff, *Capriccio Espagnol*), and Oriental scales (Mahler, *The Song of the Earth*, and Ravel, *Mother Goose* Suite).

Composers have drawn even more often on Turkish music, a sign of the military and political involvement that western Europe has had with the Turks since the Middle Ages. Turkish music consists principally of marches scored with colorful instruments: oboes, triangles, tambourines, various kinds of drums, and cymbals. Beethoven, in his image of universal brotherhood, uses a Turkish march style—complete with piccolo, triangle, cymbal, and bass drum—for one setting of his "Ode to Joy" in his Symphony no. 9. Mozart concludes his Sonata in A Major with a delightful rondo, *Alla Turca*.

Nuance

Nuances are shadings in musical expression. They give special accent or color to both single tones and longer passages. They may be obvious and pictorial, subtle, powerful, or gentle. Nuances, more than any other facet of musical composition, represent the ultimate refinement and eloquence of musical expression.

Schubert was a master of nuance, as shown in his superb song "The Erlking," set to a poem by Goethe. The poet tells the story of a father riding home through a storm with his child in his arms. The child, suffering from the cold and wind, sees an apparition, the Erlking, whom we will discover to be the embodiment of death. The Erlking first tempts the child with pretty games, but the child cries out in fear. The father tries to reassure the child, but finally the Erlking takes the child by force in death.

Schubert sets the mood immediately by a furiously driving rhythm in the piano. The hollow sound of repeated octaves in the right hand and rumbling figures in the bass suggest the various elements we see at first—wind, darkness, the rush of the father. There is a strong hint of the traditional *ombra* music here.

By subtle changes in the music Schubert manages to give the solo voice the appearance of singing four different parts: the narrator, the father, the child, and the Erlking. He mirrors the emotional values of the poetry in subtle yet telling fashion. Here are samples of each part:

EXAMPLE 9-6 Schubert: "The Erlking." The narrator.

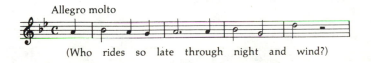

(Who rides so late through night and wind?)

First, the narrator tells of the father hurrying home through the storm and wind. The music begins in a somewhat level, matter-of-fact manner, although the agitation of the storm music in the piano tells us that this quiet manner is but a foreboding. As the narrator continues to sing, his melodic line grows active, to signify greater tension.

EXAMPLE 9-7 Schubert: "The Erlking." The father.

(My son, why do you hide your face in fear?)

The father's music is generally placed low throughout the piece, with the exception of his last phrase, when the terror of the situation seems to communicate itself to him. The sturdy interval of the perfect fourth, rising from dominant to tonic, characterizes the father's music; traditionally, it has a connotation of authority (as in a trumpet call).

EXAMPLE 9-8   Schubert: "The Erlking." The son.

(My father, my father, do you not hear?)

The child, in contrast, is given a high-pitched melodic part, of which the example above is the most characteristic excerpt. Three times we hear this outcry, each time a step higher, and each time as a refrain that answers the Erlking's persuasions. Schubert has assigned to the child's music the most unstable harmony in the piece; the pleas of the child are sung over dissonant, disturbing harmonies.

EXAMPLE 9-9   Schubert: "The Erlking." The Erlking.

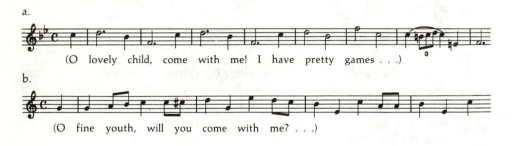

a.

(O lovely child, come with me! I have pretty games . . .)

b.

(O fine youth, will you come with me? . . .)

The two melodies of Example 9-9 represent the Erlking's music. Notice how sweet and ingratiating they are, like candy offered to a child. This is a master touch in composition, to coat the deadly intent of the Erlking with cloying sweetness. Schubert also lightens the driving accompaniment figure whenever the Erlking sings. At the very end comes the finest touch of all, as the momentum that carried throughout the piece is broken and the narrator announces in halting tones that the child is dead. Nothing could portray so well the absolute horror of the tragedy as this bare final statement.

EXAMPLE 9-10   Schubert: "The Erlking." The narrator; final measures.

Zebras by Vasarely.

10

The Experience of Form

WE HAVE DEALT WITH MUSICAL FORM already in terms of movement and arrival, the distribution of melodic material, and the layout of keys. Here we shall begin to explore it in greater depth, to approach the complete experience—the "when," "what," "where," and "how"—of musical form.

This chapter will cover the roles of rhythm, melody, harmony, and texture in what you as the listener perceive to be musical form. Chapter 11 will then apply these insights to a survey of traditonal forms. Finally, chapter 12 will look at the ways in which some specific masterworks embody the processes and layouts that have been discussed.

Rhythm as Form

Rhythm is the most basic element in musical form. Because it manages musical time, it is the common denominator for all the other processes of musical form—melody, harmony, and texture. Rhythm operates on every level of magnitude, from the simplest two-note figure to the total structure of a symphony. Rhythm is the "when" of musical form. The most pervasive role of rhythm in musical form is to mark off two kinds of time blocks: phrases and periods. In the process, rhythm performs two vital functions: it separates substantial sections for clarity, and it links them for continuity.

Phrases and periods in music have counterparts in language. A phrase is comparable to a clause in a sentence: it contains a distinct idea, but is not a complete thought. A period is comparable to a sentence, in which the thought is complete. Just as in language, phrases and periods in music have no prescribed lengths. In music associated with poetry and dance, however, phrases and periods do help arrange the musical material into a symmetry. The simplest and most familiar pattern is to link two phrases of equal length. The first phrase has an open ending;

the second phrase closes the action and finishes the period. Example 10-1, from Mozart's Sonata in A Major, is a model for this kind of form. Mozart made it totally symmetrical; if you divide it continually you will find pairings that descend to the half-measure level. On the other hand, Example 10-2, from the Haydn Sonata in E♭ Major, is most irregular. Its first two measures form a phrase that, by itself, has a certain completeness of thought but that is too short to be a real period. For balance

* EXAMPLE 10-1   Regular period. Mozart: Sonata in A Major, first movement. (On soundsheet as Example 4-3)

* EXAMPLE 10-2   Irregular period. Haydn: Sonata in E♭ major, first movement. (On soundsheet as Example 4-4)

(but not for symmetry), Haydn then plays with echo figures that make a sort of patchwork phrase. In Mozart's sonata we can predict the exact instant of arrival. In Haydn's sonata we are at the mercy of the composer, to arrive at what he considers the most telling moment. These two examples make it quite clear that a period is completed only when the music arrives at some effect of finality.

Composers project rhythm on a larger scale as they deploy events throughout a piece—striking contrasts, effective recalls of material, the spinning-out of movement or its abrupt halt. And exponentially, as we move up the scale of magnitude, we enter the world of macrorhythm: the timing of principal sections and of entire movements.

Melody as Form

Melody, the most easily recognized element in music, serves musical form as a landmark. When a composer recalls or rhymes a well-defined theme, he establishes a connection that links both appearances. By such restatements he unifies the form and makes it more intelligible for the listener (as discussed more fully in chapter 6).

Contrast of melodic ideas is another way that a composer organizes musical form. He can do this at short range, where a tug-of-war between sharply differentiated figures kicks off a long-range action (Example 6-5 illustrates such a contrast). With contrast a composer can also mark off large sections of a composition. In Example 10-3, Mahler casts the first theme in a minor key and in the rhythm of a solemn, majestic march for a dark mood. The theme inhabits the middle and lower ranges of pitch and is frequently interrupted by brief pauses. Shortly thereafter the dark mood evaporates and a completely different melody enters. The second theme flows upward, songlike and glowing, in a major key far removed from the brooding minor of the first theme, as if it came from another world and another time.

EXAMPLE 10-3   Thematic contrast in musical form. Mahler: Symphony no. 2 in C Minor.

a. First theme

b. Second theme

Melody—easily recognized by the listener due to its clear shape and specific manner—thus acts as the "what" of musical form. It is the surface of a passage, creating the profile of the ongoing action.

Harmony as Form

Harmony is involved in musical form through the location of keys in a piece. When, for example, the composer begins a piece in C major, modulates to G major, then brings the music back to close in C major, he is creating a harmonic form for his music. (This plan is sketched in Example 7-7c.) The movement to and from keys gives the music direction. Figuratively, therefore, we can say that harmony represents the "where" of musical form.

Western music for the past three centuries has based its harmonic forms on just such movements between keys. Among these movements, certain routes have taken precedence, so much so that they control most eighteenth-century music and a great deal of the music written since then. In themselves these routes are quite simple. Example 10-4 illustrates one of the preferred plans in a rather crude way. You hear four progressions, each of which by itself gives you a clear and firm sense of its key by beginning and ending on the chord that gives the key its name. The four progressions in order comprise a harmonic form that makes a tour of keys, beginning and ending in the first key. In a very simple way, this example fulfills expectations that a piece will end in the same key in which it began, thus closing a harmonic circle. As you listen to it on the soundsheet, concentrate on the bass notes. They support the harmony and give solidity to important points of arrival in each key. Notice especially those notes marked with squares. They are the tonal centers, or the "tonic" notes, for their respective keys (see also Example 7-10).

Example 10-4 makes its point painfully clear; its very roughness highlights the departure from and the return to the home key. Musically,

* EXAMPLE 10-4   Basic key scheme (major chords in capital letters; minor chords in lower case letters).

Chord: C F G⁷ C   G C D⁷ G   a d E⁷ a   C F G⁷ C
Key: C major   G major   A minor   C major

though, it won't work except as a parody. To make it work a little better, Example 10-5 smooths out the connections from chord to chord, adjusts the positions of the chords themselves, and supplies connecting links to bridge the harmonic gaps between keys. Notice also that the return to C at the end is reinforced by several more cadential effects in order to confirm the impression of final harmonic arrival. In both Example 10-4 and Example 10-5, you hear the harmony moving to a third key, A minor. This harmonic movement erases the effect of G major and raises a question as to what will follow. The music answers this question and closes the cycle of action by returning to C major.

* EXAMPLE 10-5   Basic key scheme with smooth connections.

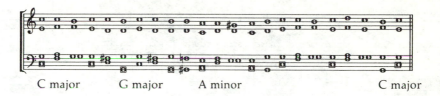

C major   G major   A minor   C major

The plan of keys given in these two examples is a virtual genetic code of harmony for the majority of compositions written from 1750 to about 1850, the principal period from which our listening repertory is taken. In this code, the first two keys are fixed: if the home key (I) is major, the second key will be V (the dominant); if the home key is minor, the second key will be III (its relative major). The third part of the harmonic plan, represented in this case by A minor, is open to many different routes, so much so that this section is best designated by the letter "x", signifying that a great number of options are available to the composer. The final section is fixed—it comes home to I. Therefore, we can symbolize the harmonic form as follows: I–V; "x"–I for the major key and I–III; "x"–I for the minor key. (The semicolon signifies the final point of arrival in the second key—an important point of punctuation—matched later on by the final point of arrival in the home key.)

The beauty of this plan is its flexibility within an unshakably firm framework. In short pieces, dances, marches, and songs it traverses its route in a short time, perhaps no more than a minute or two. But it also underpins the form of great symphonic movements, which may occupy over ten minutes. The plan can accommodate an incredible variety of melodic material. Example 10-6 presents a model of the I–V; "x"–I form, beautifully shaped by Mozart as a theme for a set of variations. This example also gives the melodic plan to show how neatly the harmonic and the melodic layouts merge.

* EXAMPLE 10-6   Model of the I-V; "x"-I form. Mozart: Sonata in D Major, third movement.

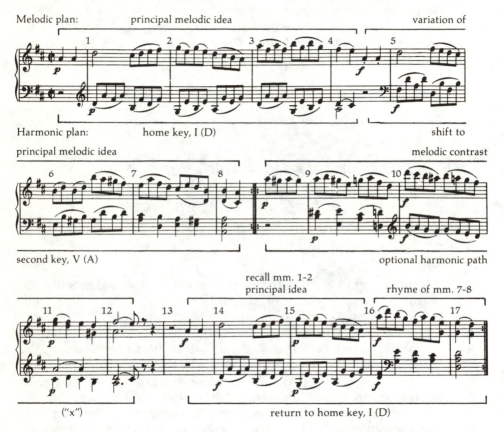

In the first movement of his Symphony no. 3 Beethoven applies the same plan on a much grander scale. Assuming that each measure takes one second, the phases of harmonic action take approximately the following amounts of time:

I	first key	40 seconds
	connection to second key	16 seconds
V	second key	one minute, 49 seconds
"x"	optional key (or keys)	
	to guide return to I	four minutes, 8 seconds
I	return to first key	five minutes. 54 seconds

Notice that Beethoven devotes more time to each succeeding principal phase. He does so in order to accomplish two objectives: to erase the impression of what has gone before and to confirm the new harmonic position. This range of proportions is particularly effective in longer works, where the composer uses them to build powerful thrusts to important points of harmonic arrival, especially the final arrival at the home key. Meanwhile tremendously rich melodic material, rhythmic manipulation, and textural play can ride upon the harmonic drive.

The I–V; "x"–I trajectory described above spans the entire form of a movement, small or large. Composers also incorporate various cycles of departure and return into sections (periods and groups of periods) within a movement. If we imagine Example 10-5, the "genetic code," expanded into the first phase of a large work, we experience all the action between the first and last chords as a presentation of the home key, an arc with its own inner crises and resolutions. The next phases of the large work, V, "x", and I, will also have their own arcs on a comparable scale. Thus the great harmonic form will emerge, with the encompassing wide arc reaching from the beginning of the piece in I to its ending in I.

Another and often more striking way a composer works with harmonic phases is to piece together several short harmonic arcs. He introduces harmonic digressions after a brief statement of the first phase, then returns rather quickly to the home key. For example, Beethoven, in the second movement of his Symphony no. 5, makes a sudden brilliant harmonic shift along with a bold change of mood from lyric to martial (see Example 10-7). He then carefully—indeed rather mysteriously—weaves a return to a recall of the first phase. He now does the same thing again, so that the greater part of the movement can be symbolized as an A B A B A form with short harmonic arcs. You can easily appreciate such bold, local changes of key, much more readily than you can follow the subtle long-range movement of keys in the

* EXAMPLE 10-7   Sudden harmonic shift. Beethoven: Symphony no. 5, second movement. (On soundsheet as Example 7-8)

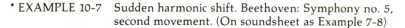

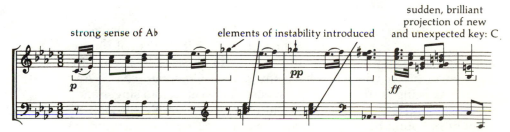

I–V; "x"–I plan. Both of these kinds of modulation play important roles in musical form, either to highlight changes of mood and color or to build a coherent harmonic form for an entire piece.

Encouraged by the richer tone qualities developed in the orchestra and the piano, composers in the nineteenth century began to concentrate on the color of harmony. Schubert was among the first to explore this harmonic resource intensively. Much of the appeal of his music lies in his luminous effects of harmony highlighted by kaleidoscopic shifts of color, as in the opening of his Quintet in C Major. As composers became more interested in effects of harmonic color, they became less bound to key-centered action. This was an effective trade-off: when you hear a striking harmonic effect, you feel little urgency for that sound to progress forward to a specific tonal center. By the turn of the twentieth century, key as a controller of form—though it still held on in much music—no longer commanded the action as completely as it had in earlier times.

Twentieth-century composers continued this movement away from key-centered harmony. The most important of these were Arnold Schoenberg and his followers and the so-called avant-garde composers of the post-World War II period: Karlheinz Stockhausen, Pierre Boulez, Luigi Dallapiccola, among many others. Béla Bartók, on the other hand, synthesized many elements from music of the past with twentieth-century techniques. His treatment of harmonic form in his *Music for String Instruments, Percussion, and Celesta* can be quickly grasped by the listener. The tonal center for the first movement is A; the harmony moves steadily away from A until it reaches E♭, then the tonal center recedes back to A. The entire form thus makes an arch. (Notice that, as a twentieth-century composer, Bartók goes to the musically distant note E♭ for his tonal contrast, instead of to the dominant, E, which earlier composers would have used.) In the finale, set in the style of a folk dance, the harmony returns several times to the home key after short, highly contrasted digressions. Thus, Bartók has adapted the two traditional harmonic plans—the long-range trajectory and the short arcs—to his own style.

Texture as Form

Texture clarifies form. It is the "how" of form. Through changes in voicing, range, tone color, and action, it marks off individual phrases and periods. This function of texture was put to use in the earliest Western music of which we have any record, Gregorian chant. As a chant was being performed, the responses between a solo singer and a group of singers articulated the form of the song simply through the amount of sound being produced. For centuries such alternations be-

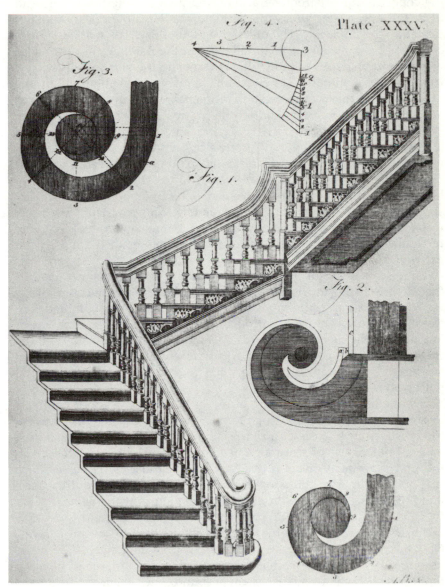

Eighteenth-century staircase design.

tween segments of an ensemble have served a clarifying purpose in musical form. One form that depended heavily on this trade-off was the concerto of the Baroque era. Its textural layout alternated solo and *tutti* (full ensemble), while the harmony circled around various keys related to the home key. The first movement of Bach's *Brandenburg* Concerto no. 2 is a model for textural layout in the Baroque concerto, with its give-and-take between the full orchestra and the four soloists: violin, trumpet, flute, and oboe. The textural contrasts are highlighted by the different tone colors of the solo instruments: suave in the violin, light and bright in the flute, brilliant in the trumpet, edgy in the oboe.

The increased range of pitch, color, and amount of sound that evolved in instruments from about 1770 onward gave Classic, Romantic, and modern composers the means to exploit textural values even more thoroughly. Beethoven gives different colors to the three presentations of his opening theme in the first movement of his Symphony no. 3: broadly singing violoncello tone; light, lyric flute tone; and powerful brass tone, respectively. All three statements are in the home key of the piece. The textural changes add a profile of color to the melody, the harmony, and the rhythm.

Large-scale works of the Romantic era carry textural distinctions further. Tchaikovsky, in the first movement of his celebrated Symphony no. 6, the *Pathétique,* supports striking contrasts of effect with bold contrasts of texture. The slow introduction is essentially a procession of low-pitched darkly colored chords proper to the lugubrious mood; the *allegro* that follows gets embroiled with a furious give-and-take; this then subsides, giving way to a broadly flowing melody supported by intensely sweet harmonies.

Twentieth-century composers also rely heavily on textural contrasts to delineate various sections of a form. Stravinsky characterizes each of the episodes in *Le Sacre du Printemps* by its own orchestration. Bartók makes brilliant use of textural values to mark off principal sections in the first movement of his *Music for String Instruments, Percussion, and Celesta.* The first two-thirds of this movement is densely contrapuntal, building a thick texture with constant imitations. At the climax of the movement, the dense counterpoint suddenly dissolves and the whole orchestra comes together on a single note, doubled in several octaves. Now the counterpoint resumes, but more sparsely until the music reaches its home key. Here the bell-like celesta enters with a spread of light, rapid notes, creating a misty curtain of sound. This veil of sound freezes the counterpoint, which then becomes like arabesque figures against a background—moving, but going nowhere. Thus, Bartók has used texture to clarify the phases of the form—departure, arrival at a point, and return to home base.

In summary, we might say that rhythm is the driving power of form, its instant-to-instant thrust; melody and texture articulate form, establishing landmarks and other topography; and harmony is the great chain, the unbroken line that goes from here to there and back again.

Whirlpools by M.C. Escher.

11

Musical Forms

A COMPOSER SETTING OUT TO WRITE A PIECE has a basic form in mind, much as a chef builds upon a basic recipe in creating a fine dish. Both composer and chef begin with good ingredients. They use a basic form or recipe to put their materials into good order and effective combinations. Finally, they add the personal touch that makes their creations works of art.

Each of the forms to be described in this chapter has served as a guideline to composition and to perceptive listening. Each form makes sense. Each provides a recipe that has been available to masters and to beginning composers alike. In the hands of an imaginative composer each form invites variant layouts, so that each composition may have its own turns of phrase, its own subtlety, its own wit. You can best appreciate a composer's felicity of invention and expression by becoming familiar with the prototypes: two-reprise form, three-part forms, rondo forms, variation, sonata form, concerto forms, fugue, and free forms.

Two-Reprise Form

In its simplest version, this form consists of two periods, each eight measures in length. These periods were called reprises in seventeenth- and eighteenth-century music, since each period was generally repeated or reprised in a thirty-two measure A A B B sequence. Many traditional songs are laid out according to the two-reprise plan (although they do not repeat each period), among them "Drink to Me Only With Thine Eyes," "Jingle Bells," and "Yankee Doodle." Popular and court dances from the medieval period to the nineteenth century were performed to music written in two-reprise form.

The beauty of this form is its clarity, balance, and economy. Being short—and usually featuring a fetching tune—it is clear. Its balance lies in the elegant statement-response relationship of its two periods. The first period ends with the impression that the music will probably continue, creating an open-ended effect. The second period ends with a final arrival, creating a solid effect of closure. The economy of the two-reprise form arises from the fact that when each short period is repeated the composer and listener get double the mileage—you hear each twice while sensing the balance that repetition promotes.

Example 11-1 from Mozart's Sonata in A Major is the first reprise of a short two-reprise form. This example ends in the home key; Mozart

* EXAMPLE 11-1   First reprise of a two-reprise form. Mozart: Sonata in A Major, first movement. (On soundsheet as Example 4-3)

Andante grazioso

adds another period just to balance the form. Example 11-2, from the first movement of Mozart's Sonata in D Major, gives both reprises. Here, the first reprise modulates to the dominant key, A major. It embodies the I–V phase of the I–V; "x"–I plan.

The shift of key in Example 11-2 raises a harmonic question: "What about getting back to the home key?" This is the task of the second reprise. After a bit of harmonic probing—"x"—a momentary pause ushers in the final bit of music that settles itself neatly in the home key, I. If you count the measures in Example 11-2 you will find that the second reprise has an extra measure (9). Mozart has done a bit of subtle juggling, stretching out the beginning of the second reprise to build an effect of suspense that makes the return of his tune especially gratifying.

Nonmodulating two-reprise forms tend to be short; their stay-at-home harmony reinforces their neat little symmetries. On the other hand, if the composer decides to shift to another key—I–V—at the end of the

* EXAMPLE 11-2   Two-reprise form, modulating to dominant key. Mozart:
Sonata in D Major, third movement. (On soundsheet as
Example 10-6)

first reprise, he opens the door to considerable room for expansion.
Example 11-3, from Bach's Suite in E Major, illustrates such expansion.
At measure 7, he reaches the dominant with a light cadence. To nail
down the effect of the dominant, however, he must continue for five
more measures before reaching a powerful cadence in measure 12. Now
the way back to the home key, "x", has to overcome the persuasiveness
of this modulation in order to make the final return home, I, convincing.
This will take some thirty measures, of which Bach devotes the last
seventeen to securing the final close in the home key.

To get some idea how Bach expanded the two-reprise form, compare
the actual piece (Example 11-3) with its reduction to the minimal sixteen-
measure form (Example 11-4). In the reduction, notice that measure 4
links perfectly to measure 9, so that measures 5-8 act as a parenthesis;
also, measure 16 links just as smoothly to measure 39, so measures 17-
38 amount to a substantial excursion and return. Despite the length of
the two-reprise form in this piece, Bach obviously had the short model
clearly in view at all times, since it represents the boundaries of the
form. (The piece itself is based on a dance, the bourrée. This bourrée,
however, is not danced; it simply reminds the hearer of the actual dance
music from which it sprung.)

What happens to the melody in a two-reprise form? Well, here the

* EXAMPLE 11-3   Extended two-reprise form. Bach: Suite in E Major, bourrée.

Example 11-3 continued

*EXAMPLE 11-4   Reduction of Example 11-3 to a 16-measure two-reprise form (with corresponding measure numbers).

composer has some additional options. He can bring back his original tune to close the form, as Mozart did in Example 11-2, or he can match endings, as Bach did in Example 11-3. Or, as in "Jingle Bells," the music can go on to something new in the second reprise. The intriguing interplay between a firm yet flexible framework and a wide range of options has made the two-reprise form a favorite for composers since the seventeenth century. Lully, Rameau, Bach, Handel, Haydn, Mozart, Beethoven, Schubert, Chopin, Mendelssohn, Schumann, and Brahms have laid out many of their short pieces and songs in two-reprise form. The form also shapes minuets, marches, waltzes, polkas—most of the traditional popular music of the past two centuries.

The two-reprise form also has modular possibilities. Like modular furniture, individual pieces can be linked, coupled in various ways to build larger works. Hence the term couplet form, which designates a piece made up of a series of these short forms.

Three-Part Form

This is the simplest coupling, an A B A arrangement, in which each letter represents a complete two-reprise form. The B section of a three-part form is designated as a trio. This term comes from the tradition of the seventeenth and eighteenth centuries to have this middle section played by a small ensemble of solo instruments, generally a trio. Beethoven's familiar Minuet in G is a model for three-part form. Each of its four periods is a trim eight measures in length, neatly segmented every two measures. Its melodies are elegant and graceful, set off against each other in gentle contrast.

In concert music you will hear three-part forms in the minuets and scherzos (this term means "joke") of symphonies and chamber music. By Beethoven's time the eighteenth-century minuet was often speeded up to become a scherzo. This second-generation minuet took on an exuberant, sometimes violent manner, with touches of humor ranging from subtle wit to pie-in-the-face slapstick, as in the scherzo of Beethoven's Symphony no. 2. For the listener, the three-part form as presented in minuet or scherzo style is the most easily grasped of all forms. In keeping with this accessibility, the music itself is usually pleasant and open, touching upon a variety of moods. For example, Mozart gave the minuet in his Symphony no. 39 in E♭ Major a stately manner. In contrast, the trio is a bucolic Ländler, a country waltz such as might be played at a peasant festival.

Because of their brevity and their neatly laid out periods, these three-part forms can etch little vignettes—scenes that appeal immediately to listeners. We hear hunting calls, pastoral tunes, courtly attitudes, bold military gestures, even effects drawn from the contrapuntal intricacies of the learned style or the supernatural shadows of the *ombra*.

The three-part form maintained its presence in the nineteenth and twentieth centuries. Johann Strauss often calls for the A B A relationship of the various reprises of his waltzes. Béla Bartók no doubt had a retrospective intention when he set the second movement of his Concerto for Orchestra, "Il Giocco delle Copie" ("The Play of Pairs") in an A B A form.

Rondo Forms

Rondo means "round" in Italian. In music it refers to a form in which a principal theme comes around again after intervening material. The principal theme is called a refrain; intervening material is designated by the term episode. In the earlier eighteenth century, rondos and their French counterparts, *rondeaux,* consisted of a chain of two-reprise forms typically coupled in this order: A B A C A D A. No specific number of alternations was prescribed, but three refrains were the general minimum for a rondo form. Some familiar pieces and their rondo layouts are:

A B A B A   Beethoven, Quartet in B♭ Major, finale
A B A C A   Haydn, Sonata in D Major, finale
A B A C B A Mozart, Concerto in A Major, finale

Of these three examples only the Haydn finale represents the older type of rondo, with coupled two-reprise forms. The Beethoven and the Mozart finales spin out their material at length. They retain the rondo effect by a solid return to the refrain after the first episode. As you may gather, rondos, with their fetching tunes often recalled, are apt forms for finales. A rondo makes a nice dessert to top off the substantial repast of a symphony or concerto.

Variation Form

Variation has two meanings in music. Every musical passage is a variation of something already at hand to which the composer aims to give fresh value. But variation is also a form, in which the composer writes a set of short pieces based upon a preexisting theme. Like the three-part form and the rondo, these pieces are coupled, forming a set of variations.

In its most familiar and attractive role, the variation form is a musical showcase, a fashion show in which the model (i.e., the theme) is the same, while the dress differs for each variation. Mozart, in the opening movement of his Sonata in A Major, gives a simple pastoral theme, then dresses up the theme with piquant embellishments (Example 6-8). He continues the variation process with other arrangements of rapid notes, several times assigning them to the accompaniment until the piece climaxes with a broadly scaled slow movement modeled after the aria (an operatic solo). Mozart's aria-like piece, like all the variations, is shaped exactly to the two-reprise layout of the theme. A quick variation in the style of a contredanse (a popular eighteenth-century dance in duple time) winds up the piece, adding a few measures for an emphatic arrival.

Variation can take on a serious note and achieve great scope. The "Crucifixus" from Bach's Mass in B Minor proceeds as a freely composed piece over a four-measure bass theme. Bach expresses the tragic mood with rich and complex contrapuntal textures and unstable harmonies (see chapter 12). Beethoven sets the finale of his *Eroica* Symphony in variation form. He adapts the form to his own individuality in the middle of the movement, though, by breaking the two-reprise mold of the theme in favor of several extended, discursive variations in the learned manner (see chapter 12).

Sonata Form

Sonata form is something of a wonder. It rose quickly to prominence around 1760–70. From that time until the early twentieth century composers cast the first movement of almost every sonata, concerto, symphony, or quartet—as well as many slow movements and finales—in sonata form. No other form has ever appeared so rapidly on the musical scene or caught on with composers of all nations so completely as did sonata form.

The term sonata means "sounded" in Italian—as distinguished from cantata, which means "sung." In the seventeenth and eighteenth centuries these terms were applied to instrumental and vocal pieces intended for home, court, or church use. In the nineteenth century, music theorists began to apply the term sonata form to the form often used in first movements of instrumental works. Nowadays, it is commonly understood to signify the form described here.

Harmonically, sonata form has the same overall shape as the two-reprise form: I–V; "x"–I. Suppose we visualize this harmonic structure as a bridge. Terra firma is represented at the beginning and the end by

EXAMPLE 11-5   Graphic representation of small two-reprise form.

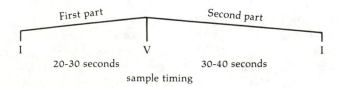

First part   Second part

I   V   I

20-30 seconds   30-40 seconds

sample timing

a solid sense of the home key. In the two-reprise form there are two spans to this bridge, anchored in the middle by a strong cadence in V, the dominant key. This is exactly how Mozart laid out the portion of his Sonata in D Major that is shown in Example 11-2. Example 11-5 shows this scheme graphically.

This is a small structure, taking less than a minute to traverse its ground. Now, imagine the same structural plan expanded to cover a much larger area—say, twelve minutes of music. The pillars would have to be anchored much more strongly and the spans would have to be strengthened and supported by subsidiary pillars. Perhaps also the bridge itself would have to be reached and left by approaches, as illustrated in Example 11-6.

EXAMPLE 11-6   Graphic representation of sonata form.

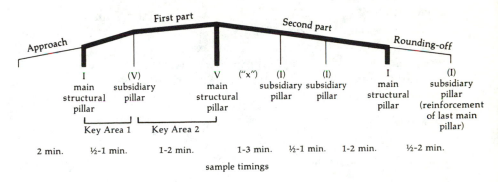

This is the game plan of sonata form, a plan composers have followed consistently, no matter what paths they may take between pillars. The brackets, marked "Key Area 1" and "Key Area 2," indicate the tonic and the dominant, which respectively comprise the harmonic sections of the first part.

The main and subsidiary pillars, along with the section marked "x", represent important stations in the form. The sections they enclose have been given names which, because of the consistency with which composers shape the general outlines of their sonata forms, fit quite well:

First Part: *Exposition*   in which the *two* keys—I (tonic) and V (dominant)—and their respective thematic material are exposed or presented.

Second Part: *Development*   in which harmonic exploration away from the two keys and thematic manipulation take place. This is the "x" section (see chapter 10).

Recapitulation   in which the home key is reestablished and confirmed by recalling and rhyming the thematic material of both key areas of the exposition, but this time in the tonic (the home key).

Coda   (optional) which acts as an added closing section for the form.

Composers imbed one or more salient themes in a sonata form. These serve as landmarks to help us get our bearings within the form. They act as areas of both arrival and departure. As we studied the small two-reprise form earlier in this chapter, we noticed how the theme, stated at the beginning of the piece in the home key, returned later to signal the reestablishment of the home key. Sonata form uses thematic material in the same way.

The I–V; "x"–I plan—both in its two-reprise and sonata-form versions—appealed to composers largely because of its sturdiness. Another advantage of the plan was its ability to embody harmonic contrast and reconciliation at long range within the sonata form. We can visualize sonata form as a debate or a test of authority. Imagine a confrontation

EXAMPLE 11-7   Melodic material. Mozart: Eine kleine Nachtmusik, first movement.

First key themes

Exposition

measure 1

m. 5

m. 11

Recapitulation

measure 76

m. 80

m. 86

Second key themes

m. 28

m. 35

m. 101

m. 108

between an emperor and a king. The emperor represents the home key (the tonic) with its own melodic material. The king represents the opposing key (the dominant) with *its* melodic material. The emperor states his initial premise, establishing the home key. The king challenges the emperor, introduces his key, and with considerable emphasis drives it home, thus achieving a temporary advantage. We have now reached the end of the second key area. The argument heats up in the development (the "x" section). The emperor's key reasserts itself in the recapitulation and eventually absorbs the melodic material of the king's key into his own realm, the tonic key, to show that it rightfully belongs at home. Mozart puts forth this harmonic–melodic action very elegantly in the first movement of *Eine kleine Nachtmusik*. Example 11-7 gives the melodic material for each key in the harmonic argument of this movement.

Concerto Form

A concerto is a composition for one or more instrumental soloists and orchestra. In an orchestral performance it is the pièce de résistance, because it features a star performer. Two kinds of concertos are familiar to listeners—the Baroque concerto and the Classic-Romantic concerto. In the Baroque era the concerto was a vehicle for brilliant instrumental performance, in which a soloist would step out from the orchestra to

EXAMPLE 11-8   Baroque concerto themes.

Bach: Brandenburg Concerto no. 2 in F Major

(Allegro)

Handel: Concerto Grosso in D Major

Allegro

Handel: Concerto Grosso in F Major

Allegro, ma non troppo

Bach: Violin Concerto in E Major

(Allegro)

do a solo turn, then step back to rejoin the ensemble. In the Baroque concerto we hear an interplay between a large group, called the *tutti* ("whole") or *ripieno* ("full"), and one or more solo instruments, called the *concertino*. This interplay between orchestra and soloist promotes a vigorous, clean-cut style and features symmetrical arrangements of short, neatly turned figures, as in Example 11-8.

The regular alternation of *tutti* and solo creates a form rather different from the two-reprise form. Instead of *opposing* two keys, the Baroque concerto *circles around* the home key—leaving it for a while, returning, leaving, returning, back and forth several times. Thus we hear both *tutti* and solo passages in various keys. This helps to maintain interest throughout the form. Example 11-9 gives the diagram of keys in the first movement of Bach's *Brandenburg* Concerto no. 2 (see also Examples 11-8 and 9-3). (The heavy black lines represent areas of harmonic stability; the thin black line represents the home key as a level of reference throughout the movement. Areas where there is no heavy black line represent shifting, relatively unstable harmonic action.)

EXAMPLE 11-9   Key scheme of Bach: Brandenburg Concerto no. 2, first
                movement.

The Classic-Romantic concerto, along with the symphony, represents the most impressive kind of instrumental music in the standard listening repertory. Many late eighteenth-century concertos maintained something of the tradition of the Baroque concerto, drawing the soloist out from the orchestra. Composers wrote concertos for clarinet, flute, oboe, bassoon, horn, trumpet, violoncello, viola, and harp. But the dramatic possibilities of the solo concerto in the late eighteenth century led composers to showcase the more brilliant and spectacular instruments, the violin and the piano, as soloists.

In his late piano concertos—those he wrote for himself to perform in Vienna—Mozart gives a panorama of concerto composition that has profoundly influenced concerto procedure for almost two hundred years. In these works we find both the lively give-and-take that characterizes the Baroque concerto and also the dramatic opposition of forces that distinguishes the Classic concerto. Further, in Mozart we meet the brilliant virtuoso soloist, the immediate predecessor of the Romantic hero-musician of the nineteenth century, as well as the ancestor of generations of composer-performers.

Structurally, concertos are laid out like other works of big scope. Generally there are three movements. The first is usually a quick piece in sonata form, modified to include an orchestral *tutti* in the tonic key at the opening, before the key area plan begins to unfold. This opening *tutti* is a theatrical strategy. It prepares the audience for the grand entrance of the soloist, much as a play or opera will frequently hold back the appearance of the main character until expectation is built up. Meanwhile, the orchestra does something very ingratiating: it presents the principal melodic material of the movement in the home key, like a preview of coming attractions. And concerto themes do tend to be attractive and somewhat more numerous than those in the usual symphonic sonata form, thereby giving the soloist opportunity to sparkle.

The middle movement of a concerto is slow and shows a close affinity with opera—specifically the aria—in the broadly singing style generally favored by most concerto composers. The finale picks up the pace again with fetching tunes laid out in rondo or variation form. One of the most delightful of Mozart's concertos is his Piano Concerto in C Major. He opens the first movement with a jaunty little march tune that quickly becomes embroiled in complex imitations. Throughout the movement he sets off this march tune against a wealth of varied melodic material—fanfares, stormy passages, singing melodies, pathetic turns of phrase—a kaleidoscope of ideas matching the lively interplay between the piano, strings, and winds. Mozart assigns the piano a number of roles: singer, brilliant soloist, and, when the orchestra takes the principal melodic material, member of the ensemble.

The nineteenth century was truly the age of the solo concerto as the brilliance of tone of both violin and piano encouraged the development of dazzling technical displays. Immense musical difficulties, excitingly conquered by the hero-soloist, astounded and captivated audiences then as they do now. The concertos of Mendelssohn, Liszt, Paganini, and, in the early twentieth century, Rachmaninoff have been test pieces for entrance into the world of the virtuoso. Brahms wrote music just as difficult into his concertos, but with a stronger and more involved eloquence. Brahms's soloist is declaiming a powerful and deeply conceived message. The figuration in his Violin Concerto in D Major is fiendishly difficult, as if Brahms wrote his concerto, in the words of one contemporary, "against the violin" instead of for it. Example 11-10 illustrates the extremely difficult figuration that runs through much of that work.

EXAMPLE 11-10 Virtuoso figuration. Brahms: Violin Concerto in D Major, first movement.

Allegro non troppo

Fugue

Fugue means "flight." In music it refers to a process in which voices follow each other in imitation. The term also refers to entire pieces written according to this process. A fugue can become very complex, a test for the skilled composer as well as for the performer and listener. Still, its origins are quite simple. We can see them today in such elementary rounds as "Row, Row, Row Your Boat." By comparing the imitation of a round with that of a fugue, we can get some idea of their similarities and differences and of how they each build their own forms.

First the round. A round is a complete melody that is neatly segmented into sections of equal length. One voice starts alone, then other voices enter in turn at the beginning of each new section. They sing the complete tune several times, then drop out as each finishes the tune after a number of turns. The harmony is simple. When all the sections are going at the same time—stacked as it were (see brackets in Example 11-11)—the sound is full, consonant, and rich.

Example 11-11 The round. "Row, Row, Row Your Boat."

```
Measures: 1  2  3     4     5     6     7     8     9     10  11   12   13   14
Soprano: Row- - -gently - - -merrily - -life - - - - - -Row- - - - -gently - - -merrily- - -
Alto:              Row- - - - -gently - - -merrily - -life - - - - - -Row- - - - -gently - - -
Tenor:                    Row- - - - -gently - - -merrily - -life - - - - - -Row- - -etc.
Bass:                          Row- - - - -gently - - -merrily - -life - - - - - -
```

A fugue is an open form, of no specified length. Unlike a round, a fugue subject need not be a complete melody; a motive with strong rhythmic-melodic imprint will do. The entries of the voices also differ from those of the round. In the round each voice enters on the same note; in a fugue the second entry transposes the subject to begin on the dominant (V). Here we have opposition of pitches, not reinforcement as in the round. The third and fourth entries reflect this opposition of pitch levels, and the I-V relationship of entries promotes the continuation of the music, rather than a circling around. Another difference: in the round the melody rigidly accompanies itself; in the fugue the counterpoint to each new entry is free of this condition, so the interactions among the voices are left to the inventiveness and skill of the composer.

A set of entries in a fugue is called an exposition. Between expositions the subject may be absent while free counterpoint proceeds. These intervening sections are called episodes. Thus, fugues simply alternate expositions and episodes. Example 11-12 shows how the opening motive of "Row, Row, Row Your Boat" could be adapted to fugal procedure.

Example 11-12 Fugal procedure.

	Exposition I								Episode			Exposition II			etc.
Measures:	1	2	3	4	5	6	7	8	9	10	11	12	13	14	15
Soprano:			Row---***************												Row---
Alto:	Row--- ********************Episode														
Tenor:				Row--- *******									Row---*****		
Bass:					Row---								Row---*****		
Entry:	on C		on G		on C		on G						on A	on E	on A

Note that ******************** represents free counterpoint.

A fugue contains at least two or three sets of entries. As each voice enters, those already in motion continue with free counterpoint (i.e., melodic material distinct from the subject yet neatly fitted to it) or one voice may remain silent.

An immense range of options is available within the general limits of key and contrapuntal imitation. Accordingly, of the 24 fugues in Bach's *Well-Tempered Clavier*, no two are alike in internal layout. To illustrate some differences, we shall look at two of the best-known pieces from *The Well-Tempered Clavier*, Fugues nos. 1 and 2.

The first fugue, a very densely woven piece of musical tapestry, is a descendant of a Renaissance genre, the *ricercar* ("to search"). Hence, the mood is serious and searching. At some points Bach has each voice enter with the subject before the preceding voice has completed its

run—a technique called *stretto* ("narrow") for its closely spaced action
(Example 11-13). The effect is to increase the intensity of musical movement. Bach calls the subject to our attention in an impressive and in-
sistent manner, so that the entire piece projects an impression of sub-
stance and importance. In this piece we can hear only two cadences,
each very powerful. The first appears about midway in the piece; the
second takes the form of a broad area of arrival, extending through the
final four measures. Throughout the twenty-seven measures of the
fugue, we hear the subject more than twenty times.

In contrast, the second fugue has a much lighter quality. It borrows
the rhythm of the bourrée, a very popular eighteenth-century dance in
quick duple time with a short upbeat. In the fugue's thirty-one measures, the subject appears only eight times. This fugue has a thin texture; its quality of movement is light and buoyant, and concern with its
subject far less serious than that of the first fugue. A very clear sense
of punctuation divides the structure into two-measure groups that tend
to form symmetrical relationships. Thus, in spite of its skillfully worked-
out counterpoint, Bach retains in this fugue the spirit of the dance that
was its source.

Free Types

Each of the set forms described so far has its own game plan, which
is outlined by keys, sections, and important points of reference. Now,
we turn to music that does not have such outlines. Even the names—
fantasia, prelude, introduction, recitative—indicate a free-flowing style,
one that wanders and changes its mood suddenly.

Generally such pieces create an expectation for a set form. An introduction sets up an expectation for a movement in sonata form, a rondo,
or a variation. An operatic recitative leads into an aria. A Bach prelude
prepares you for the fugue that will follow. Fantasias also create prep-

aration for fugues. Some fantasias are complete pieces that include both the free and the set forms in alternation. Mozart's great Fantasia in C Minor includes five parts and proceeds as follows: free, fixed, free, fixed, free (with the final free section set firmly into the home key).

Effects of freedom arise from harmonies that seem to shift without a firm footing of key, from stop-and-start motion (often with unexpected changes of style), from brilliant figuration, and from combinations of these procedures. Example 11-14 shows both the shifting harmonies and the brilliant figuration typical of the fantasia.

EXAMPLE 11-14   Fantasia figuration. Mozart: Fantasia in C Minor.

The play between set form and freedom is one of the most remarkable and exciting aspects of art music. In most of the music of the eighteenth and nineteenth centuries—symphonies, concertos, chamber music, arias, and choral works—a grand rhythm encompasses firm beginnings, strong middle points, and conclusive endings, along with a freer flow between these points. Indeed, the great Baroque, Classic, and Romantic styles are interminglings of dancelike regularity and fantasialike freedom.

From manuscript by Bach: Prelude and Fugue in B Minor.

12

Six Masterworks

WE NOW COME FULL CIRCLE. We return to several compositions recommended in the preface for listening. Applying the criteria explained in the course of this book, we will take a closer look at six of those compositions. Of the six, two are complete works—Beethoven's Symphony no. 3, the *Eroica;* and Bartók's *Music for String Instruments, Percussion, and Celesta*—and four are self-sufficient segments of larger pieces—Bach's "Crucifixus" and "Et Resurrexit" from the Mass in B Minor; Mozart's *Don Giovanni,* Act I; Chopin's Prelude no. 4 in E Minor; and Wagner's Prelude to *Tristan and Isolde.* Choral, operatic, keyboard, and symphonic media are thus represented, from the early eighteenth century to the mid-twentieth century.

Bach: Mass in B Minor, "Crucifixus", "Et Resurrexit"

The "Crucifixus" ("He was crucified") and the "Et Resurrexit" ("and was resurrected") tell of the most tragic and most joyous events in Christendom. These two pieces are the only narrative moments in the liturgy of the Mass and Bach has charged them with powerful expressive stances—extreme sorrow and high jubilation.

To convey the mood of tragedy in the "Crucifixus," Bach has gathered many musical processes that we associate with dark and pathetic moods. Example 12-1 illustrates these. The center of sound is low; the bass line controls the motion. Both in the bass and the upper voices melodic lines bend slowly downward, suggesting the head bowed in sorrow. These lines have chromatic inflections (notes foreign to the key) that color the melody; together with unstable, dissonant harmonies, they contribute to the poignant effect. Bach chose the rhythm of the sarabande—a slow, grave dance in firmly measured triple time—to frame these passages. For the bass line, he drew upon the chaconne dance form, in which the

EXAMPLE 12-1 Bach, Mass in B Minor, "Crucifixus."

bass melody repeats itself every four measures. This steady, unrelenting bass suggests the inexorable tide of events, the unrelenting judg-
ment, while the upper voices enter at different moments as if pleading.

At the very end of the "Crucifixus" Bach surprises us. We would
normally expect the piece to end in E minor, the key that has ruled so
firmly throughout the entire piece. Instead, Bach shifts subtly to a closely
related and similar-sounding key, G major. This G major, set to the
words "et sepultus est" ("and is buried") is clearly pictorial; it signifies
a final resignation, as if to say "so be it." But Bach is as much the
craftsman as the poet. As the hush that closes the "Crucifixus" dies
away, suddenly the brilliant D major sound of the "Et Resurrexit" breaks
in. To bridge the gap between these extremes of feeling Bach draws
upon the harmonic surprise at the end of the "Crucifixus." His G major
is a far more effective connection to the key of the "Et Resurrexit" than
the key of the "Crucifixus," E minor, would have been. To symbolize
the rising of Christ, Bach drives his "Et Resurrexit" melody upward in
rolling waves, exuberant with a rush of quick notes. To give an especially bright edge to the key and the theme, Bach brings trumpets and
other wind instruments into prominence. The rhythm here suggests the
polonaise, a stately yet vigorous dance current in Bach's time, with
patterns such as the following:

This dance rhythm, with its scintillating mixture of longer and shorter
notes, gives the movement a powerful lift.

The "Et Resurrexit" is quite long, yet Bach holds its melodic material closely in rein, concentrating on just a few striking motives to maintain the single jubilant mood. Nonetheless, he creates massive changes in harmonic color as the music shifts from one key to another, finally to make an extended close in the home key.

After a period of relative eclipse in the latter eighteenth century, Bach's music began to command attention again in the early nineteenth century. One work that shows strong affinities with Bach's B Minor Mass is Brahms's *German Requiem.* Its treatment of the *alla breve* and its thoroughly worked-out fugal procedure is in the great tradition of church music.

Mozart: Don Giovanni, Act I, Scene 1

This is a favorite among opera lovers. Many elements contribute to its appeal. Chief among these is the skill with which Mozart and his librettist, Lorenzo da Ponte, carry the listener on an immense swing of feeling from deep tragedy to pure buffoonery. The plot of *Don Giovanni* is quite simple. Two tragic events frame the action: (1) the midnight seduction of Anna by the Don (Giovanni) at the beginning, followed by a duel in which he kills her father, the commandant; and (2) the great "supper scene" toward the end of the opera, when the statue of the commandant returns to drag Don Giovanni down to Hell. In between, the action is mainly comedy—flirtations, escapades, mistaken identities—shadowed now and then by a reminder of the somber mood of the beginning. Throughout, the Don remains untouched, no less cavalier in the supper scene than in the opening scene when he slips away after seducing Doña Anna.

Mozart strikes a note of doom at the beginning of the overture. Using the style known as *ombra* ("shadow") in a short, powerful fantasia, Mozart evokes images of the supernatural. These are the forces that will eventually bring Don Giovanni to account. This *ombra* style will be Mozart's signal for the commandant and his statue. The overture continues with a subtle harmonic link that brings us into an effervescent section characterized by buoyant, lilting fragments of melody. These suggest the Don's lifestyle of courtship and pleasure. The overture sounds as though it will come to a brilliant close with bold fanfares, but at the very end Mozart destabilizes the harmony, bypassing the expected effect of arrival to create a quiet air of expectancy.

Now the curtain rises. We see Leporello, the Don's manservant, playing the sentry at night, pacing back and forth to a low-style march tune, grumbling and wishing he could change places with his master. Leporello's song is perky and simple, set in a light texture. Mozart introduces some deft topical nuances. When Leporello sings that he would like to play the gentleman, Mozart gives him cavalier music—hunting-horn figures with a hint of gallop in the accompaniment. Between his pacing, his grumbles, and his envy, Leporello is characterized clearly for the remainder of the opera.

As Leporello ends his song the pace quickly picks up. Don Giovanni enters, pursued by Doña Anna. She is furious because the Don, masked, has entered her boudoir at midnight to make love to her while she believed she was being approached by her fiancé, Don Ottavio. Upon discovery, the Don runs away. The scene that now ensues builds tension as Anna struggles to hold the Don and he pulls away. The music portrays their tug-of-war in a vigorous, high-style march appropriate to the high social level represented by both Anna and Don Giovanni. True to the eighteenth-century sense of formality, this march has a precisely trimmed two-reprise form, reinforced at the end by a repetition of the second reprise. This repetition drives home the fury of the scene. Mozart also throws in a delicious bit of characterization: while Anna and the Don are struggling and singing their aristocratic music, Leporello, in the background, continues with his low-style patter. Here, Mozart uses texture to complete the dramatic effect of the scene, juxtaposing anger and humor.

As their singing ends, Mozart again turns a trick of harmonic subtlety, selecting a single note as a lever upon which to shift the mood from fury to deadliness when Anna's father enters. He challenges the Don to a duel. The Don accepts. Now Mozart offers one of his rare bits of pure pictorialism, depicting the thrusts and parries of the swords by flashing figures and denoting the death stroke by a sustained dissonant chord. This pictorialism is the logical outcome of previous happenings: Leporello's back-and-forth is a routine pacing; Anna's and the Don's back-and-forth is an angry, closely joined tug-of-war; the duel is a deadly back-and-forth of swords, still more closely joined.

Following the death of the commandant, Mozart inserts one of the most startling changes of mood in all opera: a moment of cynical comedy. The Don and Leporello have fled, and in the dark they seek each other out. Their conversation, cast in simple recitative (a patterlike declamation, half-sung, half-spoken), is illustrated in Example 12-2. This kind of recitative is accompanied very discreetly by a keyboard instrument, generally harpsichord.

This dive into comedy is quickly reversed: Anna, mourning the death of her father, sings one of the most touching passages in all opera (Example 12-3). Her fragments of song—highly charged with feeling—are set in the style called accompanied or obligatory recitative, meaning that the orchestra is essential as accompaniment.

(Simple recitative is like conversation, without strong feeling, and is accompanied only by a keyboard instrument. Obligatory recitative has

EXAMPLE 12-2 Simple recitative. Mozart: Don Giovanni.

(GIO.) (Leporello, where are you?)   (LEP.) (Here I am, sir, to my shame.)   (and

you, sir?) (GIO.) (I'm here.) (LEP.) (Who has been killed, you or he?) (GIO.) (What a question!)

EXAMPLE 12-3 Accompanied or obligatory recitative. Mozart: Don Giovanni.

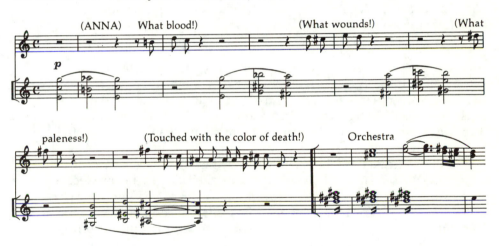

a high charge of feeling, with broken declamation, touches of figures that suggest the meaning of the text, and orchestral participation.)

The scene closes an Anna and Ottavio in a brilliant duet resolve revenge for both the seduction and the murder. The music reflects the contrasting emotions of the two. Anna begins with wild sorrow in a minor key; Ottavio consoles her, and his music shifts to a major key; the oath is sworn over shifting harmonies, and the duet closes in Anna's key as the two set their high purpose. This final number of the scene uses the dramatic elements of key contrast inherent in the sonata form, as outlined below:

HARMONIC FORM		DRAMATIC FORM
Part I	First key area, minor key	Anna sings; rejects Ottavio in her despair.
	Second key area, related major key	Ottavio offers consolation; contrast to opening mood.
Part II	Shifting harmonies	Both swear revenge; emphasis and accent of accompanied recitative.
	Return to minor; home key	Firm resolution for revenge; Anna's key and the mood of her opening music overcome the contrast of Ottavio's mood and key of consolation.

The Italian opera style that characterizes *Don Giovanni* is represented in the nineteenth century by Rossini, Bellini, Donizetti, and Verdi. In the first scene of his opera *Rigoletto*, Verdi recalls important features of *Don Giovanni*—an elegant gala, an outraged father, and a buffoon servant to a licentious nobleman.

Beethoven: Symphony no. 3 in E♭ Major, the Eroica

Beethoven's style is to thrust his music ever forward, often with a sense of intense struggle. He goes to extremes of loud and soft, explores high and low, injects startling contrasts, and builds mighty crescendos. Such gestures contribute to the tremendous scope of his Symphony no. 3, a work much longer and far more ambitious than any orchestral composition before it.

In order to create this Olympian work Beethoven merges his personal style with the principles of style and form established by his predecessors in the Classic era: Haydn, Mozart, and their contemporaries. He uses melodic topics current at his time, builds extended harmonic drives, lays out his forms by keys, and, in accordance with traditional procedure, recalls and rhymes melodic material. Eventually he brings matters into balance with a strong and final sense of arrival.

Beethoven was something of an enigma to his contemporaries because of his tendency to create feelings of uncertainty at critical points, often at the very beginning of a piece. That is exactly what he does in the first movement of the *Eroica* Symphony. After two bold opening chords he introduces a simple waltzlike melody that is easy to hum since it contains only the notes of a major triad. But in the fifth measure the tune loses its footing and sinks to a strange chromatic note. The theme eventually finds its way back to terra firma, but by then its clarity and innocence have vanished. Again and again Beethoven will start the theme, only to turn and twist it somehow. He saves its proper, simple appearance for a climactic passage toward the end of the movement, when it finally proceeds in the sing-song way promised at the beginning of the movement. Example 12-4 gives the first and last statements of the principal theme of the movement.

EXAMPLE 12-4   Beethoven: Symphony no. 3, first movement.

a. Opening theme, first statement

b. Opening theme, final statement

This treatment of the opening theme represents a huge question–answer relationship, a problem stated and eventually solved. For the listener attentive to the adventures of the theme, this can help give the movement a sense of unity beyond the relationships usually found in Classic music.

Beethoven scaled the first movement of this symphony much more broadly than any previous first movement in the history of music. Its 691 measures take more than eleven minutes to perform. This greater length grows from *within*, rather than from sections added toward the end. Two striking procedures, which can easily be recognized even at a first listening, contribute to the broader scope:

1. The movement is in quick triple time but Beethoven often throws the meter off balance by accenting a second or third beat: 1 2 3 or 1 2 3. This disturbs the sense of triple time and builds a powerful forward thrust in the music.
2. Beethoven builds to very strong points of arrival and spaces them far apart. In the phases of movement that proceed from one point of arrival to the next, Beethoven incorporates rich musical content— sometimes promising arrival, then thwarting it by some tangential motion.

Here is how the form unfolds over the movement's 691 measures:

First Movement (Allegro con brio, 691 measures)

Exposition (1–148)	Relatively short first key area (KA); very long second key area
KA I (1–37)	One theme, waltzlike, quick introduction of harmonic instability, imbalance of phrases; different instrumental colors in presentation of theme (measures 3, 15, 37); rhythmic imbalance (23–37); shift to second key (45–56), new theme
KA II (57–148)	Many short themes, frequent harmonic digressions, long periods, much rhythmic imbalance; trailing off after cadence (148–52)
Development (152–398)	Two large cycles of action
Part I (166–233)	A. Stable section (166–78), theme from measure 45
	B. Unstable (178–220), several themes combined
	A. Stable (220–36), theme from measure 46
Part II (233–397)	C. Unstable (236–84), building up to a tremendous cadential drive
	D. Relatively stable (284–337), a new theme in a distant key, opening theme in several keys, new theme restated
	E. Unstable (338–97), return to home key, extended cadential drive, suspense by understatement just before return
Recapitulation (398–556)	Recomposition of first key area, virtually literal restatement of material from original second key area: exact rhyme
Coda (557–691)	A. Another development section (557–631), using opening theme and new theme from development (D); broad drive to cadence (595–631)

B. Opening theme (631–62) presented for first time in phrases that alternate tonic and dominant in absolute symmetry, four times
C. Cadential section (663–91), quoting theme from second key area

One startling feature of this movement is the appearance of a fully formed new theme in the development, at section D in the outline given above. This is a harmonic turning point in the form, at which Beethoven begins the long journey back to the home key. He eventually brings a counterweight to this striking move by giving the principal theme its proper form and room at section B of the coda. We hear it in a straightforward sing-song layout, alternating simple harmonies as though it were a folk song. Thus Beethoven gives both the most remote harmonic area and the home key extra anchorage (see Example 12-5).

EXAMPLE 12-5 Graphic representation of Beethoven: Symphony no. 3, first movement.

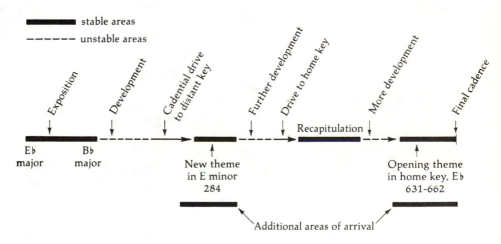

The first movement achieves its length by compressing events, with a resultant explosion of action. The second movement, in contrast, is a funeral march: it stretches out events, building its great length by a very deliberate unfolding of action. Here we have the slowing down of time. There are instants when everything seems suspended.

In the extremely deliberate motion of the funeral march—activated yet held in check by rhythms that signify muffled drums—the filling out of a two-reprise form takes considerable time. Beethoven adds another dimension to this form: he breaks off the march upon its return and leaps to another plane of action. The notes gradually become quicker and more concentrated until we have a virtual hurricane of action. Then, suddenly, there comes an interval of almost dead quiet like the eye of the hurricane (measures 154–58). The storm quickly breaks in again with renewed violence, which will gradually subside during the restatement of the march. Beethoven is not yet finished, though. He replaces the cadence that might have ended the piece at this point with a deceptive cadence that leads into the final phase. The process of expansion continues until the last measures, where the march theme is broken into fragments, punctuated by intervals of total suspension of action—a final tragic gesture.

Second Movement (Marcia funebre: Adagio assai, 247 measures)

A. (1–68)	A very slow funeral march in two-reprise form (each part repeated with some changes) followed by a concluding cadential section; minor key
B. (69–101)	A contrasting trio, also in two-reprise form (with neither part repeated), in a lyric style, interrupted by fanfares that provide a rhyme for the two sections
A.' (105–13)	Fragmentary return to the march, as if to round off the form
C. (114–73)	A developmentlike section, beginning with imitative polyphony on a new theme
A." (174–209)	Return of the march
Coda (209–47)	Cadential section for the movement, first digressing harmonically and using a new theme, then returning to a fragmentary restatement of the march

In the third movement, the scherzo, Beethoven again goes beyond the typical Classic contrast of slow movement to quick movement. He releases pure energy in a headlong drive. He announces a problem in the first reprise, barely touching on the home key and throwing the phrase structure off balance with groups of six, five, and three measures. The rest of the scherzo works toward clarification—a triumphant affirmation of the home key and a nailing down of the four-measure phrase structure. The trio features a delightful horn fanfare, a simple tune that contrasts with the restless rush of the scherzo.

Third Movement (Scherzo: Allegro vivace, 442 measures)

Scherzo (1–166)   Reprise I (1–28)
                          Reprise II (29–166)

Trio (167–255)   Reprise I (167–97)
                          Reprise II (198–255)

Scherzo da capo and coda (256–442)

In the fourth movement, Beethoven returns to what we might call the real world of musical time and movement. The piece is a set of variations built upon a contredanse tune and its bass line (Example 12-6). Beethoven had used these before as melodic material in several compositions. He characterizes the sections of his movement according to familiar topics, as the outline shows.

EXAMPLE 12-6   Contredance tune and its bass line. Beethoven: Symphony no. 3, fourth movement.

Fourth Movement (Allegro molto, 473 measures)

Opening flourish (1–11)

Home key   { 1. Decorative variations on the bass (12-75)
              2. The melody with ornamental garlands (76–107)
              Transition (107–16)

Other keys { 3. A fugal passage on the bass subject (117–74)
              4. A dance, using the melody (175–98)
              Transition (198–210)
              5. A march, using the bass (211–56)
              6. A songlike variation, using the melody (257–77)

Home key   { 7. A fugal passage, on the bass, with the melody
                 chiming in (277–348)
              8. A slow aria, using the melody (349–80)
              9. A grand chorale, using the melody (381–96)

Coda (397–473); return of opening flourish (431–34)

After the chorale (mm. 381–96) Beethoven abandons the variation procedure. He is making a coda, thus we hear some free harmonic exploration preparing the final exultant cadential section. The movement concludes with fanfares and rushing passages, incorporating the exciting flourish that began the movement.

As you can see, Beethoven is not content merely to put together a set of interesting elaborations on his subject. He gives the form a broad overall structure and stakes out large key areas: tonic, shifting keys, tonic. Also, cadences are often not clear-cut, thus two neighboring variations can be linked without a break. As with so much of Beethoven's music, the whole piece is based on broad gestures, violent drives, and grand ideas. Beethoven's grand manner in general and the expansiveness of this symphony in particular were touchstones for later symphonic composers of the nineteenth century, among them Brahms, Bruckner, Mahler, and Franck. Their symphonies are very broadly conceived and their manner carries an air of great portent.

Chopin: Prelude no. 4, in E Minor

In this exquisite miniature, Chopin invokes a rare mood of melancholy. The prelude's dark color, restless and unstable harmonies, slow and steady drop into lower and darker pitches, obsessive restatement of a simple two-note melodic figure—all combine to fix the mood. Yet, for all its intensity, this piece has an effect of understatement. It hints rather than allow itself to be swept away by the feeling of sadness. Example 12-7 gives the entire prelude, showing the various phases of action and points of punctuation.

* EXAMPLE 12-7   Chopin, Prelude no. 4 in E Minor.

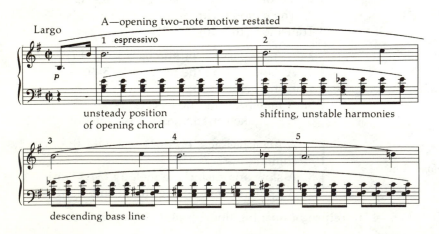

Example 12-7 continued

The piece consists of a single period, a sentence. It is divided formally in the twelfth measure by a decisive half cadence, a semicolon. Both phrases of the period begin alike, with the same melody, in the eighteenth-century tradition of popular dance and song music. The piece ends with an emphatic, clear, and final authentic cadence. Thus, at its perimeters, this prelude has a firm traditional set of boundaries which channel the fluid motion. Chopin's critical decision was to start the piece on a somewhat unsteady position for the first chord, which initiates the slow downward slide.

The bass sets us up to expect the arrival reached in measures 10–12. The bass sets us up again in the second phrase (beginning in measure 13) to expect another cadence as it moves downward, but instead the music explodes with an intense outburst of feeling, using quick notes, expressive turns, and a sudden melodic peak. Just as quickly the action subsides. It returns to its original mood and figure, and ends at the lowest level of pitch and with the darkest color in the piece.

Through his careful maintenance of structure, his steady control of melodic and harmonic direction, and his subtle deployment of harmonic color, Chopin has given exquisite shape and symbolic meaning to one of his most touching and pathetic moments. Chopin's miniatures, with their exquisite piano sonorities, are matched in the early twentieth century by Claude Debussy's short piano works, his Preludes, Books 1 and 2. Both composers rank among the most effective writers for keyboard in the entire repertory.

Wagner: Prelude to Tristan and Isolde

Wagner builds an all-enveloping mood in this piece that draws his listeners completely into the magic world of the ill-fated lovers, Tristan and Isolde. He does this at the very outset by setting up an intensely rich and restless climate of sound. The very first chord draws us into the mood of longing, frustration, and unhappiness. Rich and dark in color, this chord has an unsettling quality, a highly charged dissonance that begs for resolution. But you will hear no resolution, only a flow of unstable chords linked smoothly in an ongoing stream. At first the motion is broken by silences, but then the flow surges onward and upward to reach a shattering climax. After this highpoint, the music collapses to prepare for the rise of the curtain.

At the beginning of the prelude, Wagner implies movement in the restlessness of the harmonies rather than spell it out by a definite beat. He starts out with a slow tempo and a tentative stop-and-start pace. As the music proceeds, though, he finally reveals a more definite meter— a slowly swinging triple time—as the melodic lines merge and overlap.

Wagner's long spun-out melodic lines, with their rise and fall in gracefully balanced curves, create wavelike patterns that climb gradually to a climax then drop suddenly to resume their upward thrust. This rise and fall, matched by the build-up and drop of intensity, is called the dynamic curve. It parallels the ebb and flow of human feeling and is one of the principal reasons why Wagner's music is so compelling.

Wagner builds the long melodic lines from varied repetitions of short, well-turned motives. While we recognize these as different motives, we also sense that they have a consistency of pattern among themselves—principally stepwise motion balanced against a striking leap—and that they frequently resemble each other. This consistency promotes the flow of the melody as the motives merge smoothly. Example 12-8 illustrates the similarity of motives in the piece.

EXAMPLE 12-8   Melodic and rhythmic similarities in Wagner: Prelude to Tristan and Isolde.

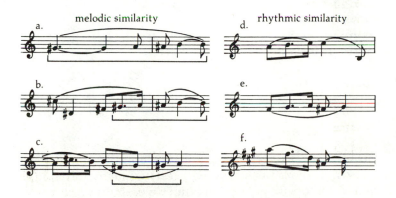

Example 12-9 sketches the first seventeen measures of the prelude, showing how motives are restated in varied form and how the melody builds to an apex in measure 13.

The entire prelude is built as one huge dynamic curve, reaching a powerful climax near the end, then dropping back quickly to the quiet stop-and-start movement with which it began. Within this great curve, certain points can be felt as stations along the way. Principally deceptive cadences that echo the gesture of measure 17, these also represent the peaks of smaller dynamic curves within the form (Example 12-10). The only authentic cadence among them occurs at measure 24, but the melodic action rides on past this point.

EXAMPLE 12-9   Opening melodic layout. Wagner: Prelude to Tristan and Isolde.

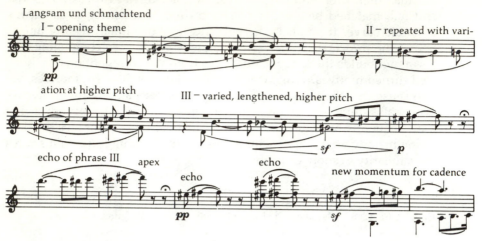

Example 12-10 Structural outline of the Prelude to Tristan and Isolde (underlinings indicate degrees of intensity).

Peaks of the dynamic curve:	measures	17, 24, 44, 62, 74, 83
Cadences:	measures	17, 24, 44, 74, 94
Key:		A A C♯ A A

Wagner's melody helps us keep our bearings within the prelude. We hear the half-dozen or more salient motives restated many times and, at the final climax, the opening motive is thundered out by the horns as if to close the melodic circle. Beyond these restatements, we hear entire phrases reiterated in varied form. For example, the phrase of measures 17–22 returns at measures 32–36, 55–58, 58–63, and 75–78.

As Example 12-10 shows, the tonal center of the prelude is A. Yet Wagner never states a strong confirming cadence in this key. The harmony constantly circles around as if it were orbiting, but never actually draws to a landing.

Often the Prelude to *Tristan* is paired in concert performance with the final scene of the opera, the "Liebestod" ("Love-Death"). These two end pieces join beautifully: the last note of the prelude links to the beginning of the "Liebestod" as a deceptive cadence. Expressively, the prelude projects the longing and sadness of the lovers; the "Liebestod" represents their fulfillment in death.

Since the harmony of the prelude is principally unstable, while that of the "Liebestod" has a strong flavor of major harmony, the overall effect when these are performed in concert is that of a large-scale cadence. This impression is reinforced by the rhythmic contrast, from irregular phrase structure to basically symmetrical structure, as we hear in the first four measures of the "Liebestod." While the prelude has a complex chain of motivic layouts, the "Liebestod" builds its great dynamic curve with two principal figures: the opening songlike motive and the final cadential motive, repeated and extended to reach an ultimate climax. After this, the scene and the opera reach a close with a magic transformation of the opening measures of the prelude (see Example 6-7), extended to reach an intensely poignant cadence that fades slowly into silence. Example 12-11 quotes these three principal melodic elements of the "Liebestod."

EXAMPLE 12-11 Principal melodic materials. Wagner: Tristan and Isolde, "Liebestod" ("Love-Death").

a. Opening melody

b. Cadential figure

c. Transformation of beginning of prelude into cadence

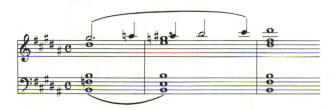

Wagner was one of the most influential composers who ever lived. His harmonies, rich and colorful, became an important source for musical impressionism (Debussy and Ravel); his constant tensions led to musical expressionism (Mahler, Schoenberg, Berg, Webern).

Bartók: Music for String Instruments, Percussion, and Celesta

Each of the works discussed in this chapter has been a synthesis of style features current during the composer's time. This work, too, is such a synthesis. In one respect, Bartók's accomplishment is the most remarkable of all, for he brings together features from styles that are widely divergent.

At the time he wrote the *Music for String Instruments, Percussion, and Celesta,* the late 1930s, the musical scene was alive with different trends. Claude Debussy and Maurice Ravel had defined impressionism; Arnold Schoenberg, Alban Berg, and Anton Webern had evolved the twelve-tone school that emerged from expressionism; Igor Stravinsky had defined the modern folkloric style and was deeply into his neoclassic period; Jan Sibelius and Sergei Rachmaninoff were still writing in a late Romantic idiom; Edgard Varèse was the great experimenter; jazz had evolved from New Orleans style through various phases to the Big Band style; some elements of exotic music, from Africa and Asia, were being absorbed in Western art music. For his *Music for String Instruments,* Bartók borrows elements from each of these trends. He places them side by side at times, blends them together at times. He produces a model of clarity and unity, one of the great works of musical neoclassicism.

The first movement combines elements of Baroque, Romantic, twelve-tone, and impressionist styles. It is a fugue, worked out very tightly. It is built upon the principle of the dynamic curve similar in contour to Wagner's Prelude to *Tristan and Isolde.* Its imitative entries move systematically through the twelve tones of the chromatic scale (i.e., all the notes, black and white, on the piano). Toward the end of the movement

EXAMPLE 12-12   Graphic representation of Bartók: Music for String Instruments, Percussion, and Celesta; first movement.

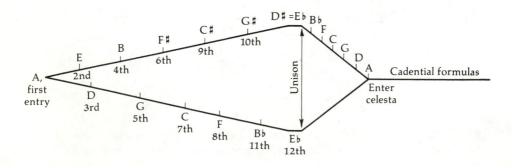

Bartók introduces an atmospheric effect, drawn from impressionism, to stabilize the movement and prepare for final arrival. The plan of the fugue is not only impressive, it is unique. Example 12-12 shows its outline. The most remarkable feature of this movement is the effectiveness with which Bartók directs movement forward to strong points of arrival. Notwithstanding the thoroughly dissonant harmony, a sense of progressing tonal centers is present. The entries of the subject explore systematically all the tonal centers of the chromatic scale. The two streams of harmonic movement describe a full circle and converge upon the tonal center E♭—the point musically farthest away from the original tonal center, A. At this point the polyphonic texture disappears and a powerful unison hammers out the E♭—the tone of arrival and the climax of the form. Reversing the build-up, the music returns to the original tonal center, A, in more relaxed fashion. It will be the final area of arrival in the movement.

Upon reaching it, the music undergoes a striking change in texture. The celesta—a keyboard instrument with a bell-like sound—enters for the first time. An impressionistic curtain of sound created by the celesta and by shimmering strings introduces an element of textural stability not previously heard in the piece. The entries now begin and end on the tonic, giving the effect of cadential formulas.

As he frequently does, Bartók uses wedge shapes in this movement. In a wedge plan there is a point of departure, generally the tonal center that represents stability. The music progresses by stages away from this center and then returns. The diagram of the form given in Example 12-12 shows a typical wedge formation. The cadential formula at the end of the movement represents this configuration. It moves from A to E♭ and then back to A. The second movement represents an electrifying contrast to the first. It is principally a dance, based on short, vigorous motives. The harmony, in contrast to the complete chromaticism of the first movement, is basically diatonic (using only notes that belong to the key), with polytonal elaborations (suggesting two or more tonal centers at the same time). The movement is in a clearly defined sonata form, as is shown in the following outline.

First key area	C	measures 1–19
Transition		20–68
Second key area	G	69–185 (cadences in G, 180–85)
Development		187–372
Recapitulation		373–520
Material of second key area at measure 412 recalled, rhymed		

Baroque stage design by Andrea Pozzo.

The key definition in the form is obvious; repetitions and cadences involving the tonal centers leave no doubt about harmonic points of reference. The principal expressive value is the dance quality. As such, then, this movement is quite in the spirit of a Beethoven or a Haydn sonata form. Moreover, the texture and part writing show the active manipulation of motives and the energetic contrasts that characterize Classic style.

Following the down-to-earth style of the second movement, Bartók opens the third movement with one of the most unexpected and weird effects in all music: the sound of the xylophone tapping away by itself. A bit later another disembodied texture—created by totally different figures in viola, timpani, and xylophone—suggests expressionism. The entire movement is concerned with curious effects of sonority, and therefore recalls impressionism. The form, like the first movement, is a wedge, this time worked out like a mirror structure.

A. Improvisation	1–19
B. Lyric melody first presented, then treated contrapuntally	20–44
C. Bell-like motive, treated percussively in many variations of texture	45–62
B. Return of lyric melody	63–75
A. Return of improvisation	76–83

Bartók, in this movement, has managed to keep the cadential sense very clear. This helps to bind the highly contrasted episodes into a smoothly continuous form. Each succeeding episode seems to come as a point of arrival, a cadential resolution to the movement of the preceding section.

The finale is a folk dance, an exhilarating summary of the entire piece. The syncopations (accents on off-beats) and cross-rhythms of folk music permeate the entire piece. The form is episodic, with rondolike refrains; contrasts are sharp; and the melodic material is well defined, as dance tunes should be. An interesting and amusing detail of style occurs in measures 262–70, where Bartók slips into a typical jazz break by giving a fresh nuance to the syncopations of his refrain theme. Throughout this last movement the sense of tonal center is more clear than in any previous movement. One might say, then, that it is the harmonic area of arrival for the whole composition—a relationship quite proper for a neoclassic concept.

The four movements of this work exhibit relationships between themselves that give the entire composition a special unity. We hear the subject of the opening movement in each of the succeeding movements: briefly and varied in the second movement; restated and developed at length in the B sections of the third movement; and altered harmonically in the fourth movement to create a bolder, more diatonic effect, in keeping with the more open and assertive manner of the movement. Further, the four movements of the piece work in pairs: the first and third (with their qualities of instability) assume the wedge form, while the second and fourth (with their powerful rhythmic drives) are organized respectively as sonata form and rondo. It is only in the last movement that the tonal center A, indicated in the first movement, is vigorously embodied with a strong flavor of the major key.

Epilogue

In exploring the musical experience we have come a considerable distance, from first impressions of sound, movement, and arrival to a perception of the grand plan, the complete form of a musical composition. These two focal points of our experience—first impression and perception of design—reinforce each other. We get some idea how the piece may unfold by the qualities of sound and movement which the composer offers at the outset. Design carries these along to give the piece shape and scope, so that our first impressions can be effectively linked to what we hear later on.

Of these two focal points, impression is the fundamental. Everyone who experiences music—listener, performer, composer—starts from the same place: sound or movement that implies feeling or image. As one who has dealt with these experiences in the role of teacher as well as listener, performer, and composer, I have found that the surest way to grasp the essential qualities of a piece of music is to return constantly to those basic impressions, to see how they rule the shape of the piece. As long as you are in tune with these impressions you can proceed as far as you wish along lines of technique and form. You may be content with first impressions; you may recognize some aspects of the grammar of music; you may appreciate its form. But ultimately, each of these stages rests upon the fundamental ability of music to stir the feelings and to move the spirit.

Appendix

How to Read Music

Even if you do not read music, you can make some sense out of many of the musical examples in this book just by looking at the patterns of the notes: their rise and fall, their density, and so on. But to get more out of the examples, you should understand the basics of musical notation. You can hear many of the examples on the soundsheets that come with this book. If you wish to explore even further the effects created in the examples, you may play them yourself on the piano, for which these examples have been arranged. Even if you have never played a musical instrument, it can be an exciting and rewarding experience to produce a simple passage at the piano, bringing to life the effects symbolized by the notation.

Pitch

Musical pitch is indicated on a five-line graph called the staff. Signs called clefs are placed at the left-hand edge of each staff to be used as guides for locating specific notes. Two clefs are most commonly used: (1) the F or bass clef, with two dots surrounding the fourth line upward on the staff to locate the note F *below* middle C (see Example A-1); and (2) the G or treble clef, which curls around the second line of the staff to locate the note G *above* middle C. (A third clef, called the C clef, notated as , is presently used in orchestral and chamber music for instruments in the lower middle range, i.e., alto and tenor levels. This clef designates the note middle C.) Other notes are reckoned upward and downward from the clef notes; each line or space on the staff represents a specific pitch level, depending on the clef sign being used. Example A-1 shows a staff with both clef signs, a section of a piano keyboard, and the notes on the staff that correspond to the white keys of the piano. Note especially the arrows that locate the clefs on the staff.

EXAMPLE A-1   Clefs and their positions on the piano keyboard.

a. Staff and clefs

b. Section of piano keyboard

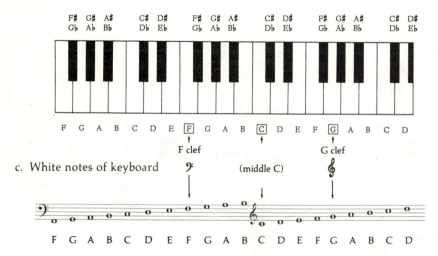

c. White notes of keyboard

The distance from one note to another is called an interval. The interval from C to D, for example, is a second; from C to E is a third; C to F a fourth; and so on (Example A-2). If you start on any piano key and play the white notes moving upward (to the right), you will notice that the intervals between the notes are of two different sizes. The intervals between E and F and between B and C are *smaller* than the

EXAMPLE A-2   Intervals.

others. The smaller intervals are called half steps; the larger are whole steps. The black keys provide half steps between the white whole steps. A line of notes moving upward or downward stepwise is called a scale.

Time

When the composer writes tempo instructions for the performer, he establishes a time value for one type of note. The time values for the other notes are then played as multiples or dividends of that one. For example, if a half note is supposed to be, say, two seconds in length, then a whole note will require four seconds, a quarter note one second, and an eighth note one-half second. If the composer writes a dot after a note, the performer increases the duration of that note by half. Examples A-3 and A-4 illustrate the relative lengths of the various notes, based on a half note of two seconds in duration.

EXAMPLE A-3   Relative durations of notes.

EXAMPLE A-4   Durations of dotted and nondotted notes.

At the beginning of a piece, to the right of the clef on the first staff, there is a figure that looks like a fraction, such as $\frac{4}{4}$, $\frac{6}{8}$, etc. These are time signatures. They designate the number of notes of a given value that are to be included in the time unit called the measure. Thus a time signature of $\frac{4}{4}$ specifies that each measure in the piece will be four quarter notes in length (unless the time signature is changed in the course of the piece). This length may be made up from notes of various lengths— half notes, quarters, eighths, etc.—but all the notes in a measure will add up in length to four quarters. Measures are marked off by vertical bar lines. Example A-5 illustrates some of the more commonly used measure lengths (or meters), based on the patterns of familiar melodies. (Notice that some pieces, such as "Home, Sweet Home" and "Oh, Susanna," begin with one or more short notes before the first full measure. These are called pick up notes.)

EXAMPLE A-5 Measures.

a. Home, Sweet Home

Be it ev - - er so hum - - ble, there's no place like home

b. Oh, Susanna

I came from Al - a - ba - ma with my ban - jo on my knee

c. America

My coun - try, 'tis of thee, Sweet land of lib - er - ty

d. Silent Night

Si - lent night! Ho - - ly night! All is calm, all is bright.

Example A-6 may be helpful as a simple application of the notation principles described above. If you have a piano, play the notes given in A-6a, using the picture of the piano keyboard as a guide. Then, tap out the patterns of note length given in A-6b. Finally, put the two together to play part of "Jingle Bells."

EXAMPLE A-6 Notation of "Jingle Bells."

a. Pitch

b. Note lengths

c. Pitch and note lengths combined

Jingle bells, jingle bells, jingle all the way; oh what fun it is to ride in a one-horse open sleigh —

Silence is also a part of music. A line of notes may be interrupted by moments of silence called rests. These correspond in length to the note values given in Example A-3. They are notated as shown in Example A-7.

EXAMPLE A-7 Notation of rests.

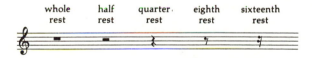

Glossary

accidental: A prefixed sign that alters the pitch of a note. (See natural, sharp, flat.)

aria: A composition for solo singer and accompaniment, generally of considerable length, with much melodic elaboration.

arrival: The point at which a phase of movement reaches an end or is marked off from the succeeding phase. This may be a pause or a cadence; it may arrest movement partially or completely.

augmented triad: A three-note chord consisting of an augmented fifth and a major third above the lowermost note.

authentic cadence: The strongest harmonic effect of arrival. It involves the dominant chord (with its root in the bass) moving to the tonic chord.

beat: A pulse or stroke that, in a series, helps establish the quality of movement, involving pace and accent.

bourrée: A popular dance of the Baroque era, in quick duple time, with a short upbeat.

brass instruments: A family of instruments, constructed of metal; producing their tones by lip vibration against a metal mouthpiece. The family includes cornets, trumpets, French horns, trombones, and tubas. The bugle is also a brass instrument.

brilliant style: Rapid passages for virtuoso display.

cadence: A pause or stopping point, usually applied to a harmonic progression.

cantata: Literally, a "sung piece." A composition, sacred or secular, for soloists and/or chorus and instruments, containing a series of vocal and instrumental numbers.

chaconne: A dance in moderately slow triple time, used characteristically as a pattern for a series of variations. The element might be a melodic line, a harmonic progression, or a recurrent bass line.

chord: A combination of three or more notes sounding at the same time.

chromatic: Refers to a note modified by an accidental. (See natural, sharp, flat, chromatic scale.)

chromatic scale: The scale that uses all twelve notes of the octave (white keys and black keys on the piano), as, for example, from D to C♯.

clef: A sign placed upon a staff to locate the position of notes. Originally these signs were letters: G above middle C, middle C, and F below middle C. The clefs presently in use are treble (G on second line), alto (C middle line), tenor (C on fourth line), bass (F on fourth line).

coda: Literally, "tailpiece." A section at the end of a movement, intended to provide a satisfactory summing up and conclusion.

concerto: An extended composition for solo instrument or instruments and orchestra, usually in three movements.

consonant: A relative term, generally equated with harmonic stability or euphony; applied to harmonic intervals.

contredanse: A quick dance in duple time, often used in finales.

counterpoint: The placing of distinctive musical lines against each other simultaneously.

deceptive cadence: A cadence in which the expected chord of resolution is displaced by some other harmony, leaving the ear not quite satisfied, requiring further cadential action.

détaché: Performed so that the successive notes are separated clearly from each other but not markedly so. (See legato, staccato.)

development: Working over of melodic material by (1) breaking it up into its motives, (2) reforming motives into new phrases, (3) changing the shape of motives, (4) directing the harmony into shifting key patterns. These procedures are usually found in the section following the exposition of a sonata form, but they are constantly used in almost any large composition. Specifically, the "x" section of a sonata form.

diatonic scale: A scale of seven different notes, containing five whole steps and two half steps arranged so that the half steps are placed a fourth or fifth apart. The effect of a diatonic scale is one of evenness and balance.

diminished triad: A three-note chord consisting of a diminished fifth and a minor third above the lowermost note.

dissonance: A relative term, generally equated with harmonic instability, or sometimes with disagreeable or unpleasant sound; applied to harmonic intervals.

dominant: The fifth degree of a scale or key (for example, G is the dominant in the key of C); the chord built upon the dominant degree.

downbeat: An accented note usually found at the beginning of a measure or on a normally stressed beat.

dynamic curve: A means of organizing a large section of music by constant growth in tension, generally leading to a significant climax or, conversely, by constant decrease to a point of minimum action.

dynamics: The strength of sound. Dynamic signs tell the performer how loud or soft to play.

enharmonic: Refers to the notation of a note in two possible ways, for example, as G♯ or A♭. Though given different names in different contexts, they have the same pitch.

episode: In rondo form, a section contrasting with the principal theme or refrain.

exposition: In sonata form, Part I, comprising first and second key areas.

expressionism: An early twentieth-century school of composition concerned with expression of strongly subjective feelings, often reflecting subconscious imagery; characterized by freely treated dissonances, angular melodic lines, irregular rhythms, and sparse texture.

fantasia: A work of improvisatory character, usually for keyboard (piano, harpsichord, organ); brilliant virtuoso passages, harmonic explorations, irregular qualities of movement.

flat: A sign (♭) that lowers by a half step any note before which it is placed.

fugue: Literally, "flight"; hence, a composition in which voices follow or chase each other. Strictly speaking, fugue is a process in which a theme or subject is presented and worked over in contrapuntal imitation by two or more parts. This process lent its name to pieces so composed.

gavotte: A French dance in moderately quick duple time; it typically begins in the middle of a measure, with an upbeat of two quarter notes; well-marked divisions in the phrasing to reflect the steps of the dance itself.

gigue: A quick dance in $\frac{6}{8}$ or $\frac{9}{8}$, often treated imitatively. English in origin.

harmony: The element of music that deals with the relationships notes can form with each other.

homophonic: Pertaining to music in which one principal melodic idea is stated at a given time.

imitation: The taking up of the subject or melody by successive voices in turn; said of polyphonic music.

impressionism: A musical style in which subtle textures and colors were used to convey impressions of the physical world, such as the play of light, air, or water; also to suggest exotic, nostalgic, and sentimental subjects.

interval: Distance between two notes. Intervals are named according to the staff degrees they encompass. Thus a second covers two degrees (for example, C to D); a third, three (C to E); etc. Intervals are further qualified according to their exact size.

key: A tonal center, generally one defined by cadential (leading-tone) action; the system of notes governed by a given tonal center, such as C major, F minor.

key area: A section of a composition centering upon one key.

Ländler: A German dance in triple meter, similar to the waltz, but with some elements of the minuet.

leading tone: Ordinarily, the seventh degree of the major scale or the (raised) seventh degree of the minor scale.

learned style: In later eighteenth century, contrapuntal composition.

legato: Performed in a smooth manner, without noticeable break in sound. (See détaché, staccato.)

leitmotif: A significant motive, which may have a distinctive melodic, rhythmic, or harmonic quality and which is assigned to some idea, person, or situation.

major scale: A scale in which the order of whole steps and half steps is: 1 1 ½ 1 1 1 ½.

mazurka: Polish dance in quick triple time, with strong accent on beat 2 or 3.

measure: A group of beats marked off on a musical score by a vertical line.

meter: Grouping of beats into small, recurrent units. Simple duple meter involves two beats; simple triple involves three beats; compound duple involves four or six beats subdivided into two subgroups of two or three each; compound triple involves triple division, the subgroups containing two or three beats each.

middle C: The note C at the midpoint of the piano keyboard.

minor scale: Scale characterized by the interval of a minor third between scale degrees 1 and 3 (for example, between C and E♭). The "natural minor scale" has the following order of steps and half steps: 1 ½ 1 1 ½ 1 1. In order to make the minor scale effective cadentially, the seventh degree was made a leading tone with the following order: 1 ½ 1 1 ½ 1½ ½. This "harmonic minor scale" had to be adjusted to eliminate the awkward melodic interval between 6 and 7. Therefore, in the "melodic minor scale" the order is as follows: 1 ½ 1 1 1 1 ½.

minor triad: A three-note chord, consisting of a perfect fifth and a minor third above the lowermost note.

minuet: A dance of French origin, in triple meter, with a moderately quick yet elegant and graceful quality of movement.

modulation: A formal shift of tonal center, usually confirmed by an authentic cadence in the new key.

motive: A melodic fragment, two notes in length or longer, which gives a distinct impression of manner or style.

musette: A pastoral style with a sustained bass note and a simple melody.

natural sign: A sign (♮) that cancels the raising or lowering effect of a previous sharp or flat.

octave: An interval consisting of five whole steps and two half steps. The most consonant interval in music, since the two notes sound as upper and lower duplicates of each other.

ombra: Music that accompanies or suggests scenes of the supernatural.

oratorio: A dramatic representation of a religious or thoughtful subject, using many of the techniques of opera.

ornamentation: The art of adding figures to a given musical text, a process that was already in operation during medieval times and that is still in use today.

perfect fifth: An interval encompassing five scale degrees, containing three whole steps and one half step. The perfect fifth is one of the strongest embodiments of harmonic stability.

period: A section of music, generally consisting of two or more phrases, ending with a full or conclusive point of arrival and containing a rather fully expressed musical idea.

phase of movement: A musical statement whose progress forward is marked off and controlled by points of departure and arrival. Phases of musical movement are variable in length.

phrase: A fairly short section of music with a well-defined point of arrival, containing clearly formed ideas, yet lacking something in form or sense to be complete.

pitch: The level of musical sound, based on the number of vibrations given out by any specified note; how high or low a note is.

polonaise: A Polish dance, much favored in the seventeenth and eighteenth centuries; quick triple time, accent on second beat.

polyphonic: Pertaining to music that employs counterpoint.

prelude: An introductory piece, generally for keyboard; a piece in an improvisatory style.

recapitulation: In sonata form, the section following the "x" in which the material of the exposition is presented in the home key to resolve the harmonic contrast first established. It acts as a rhyme to the exposition.

recitative: Musical declamation, usually in opera, in no set meter or rhythm; echoes the inflections of speech.

refrain: The principal theme of a rondo. More generally, a section that returns periodically in a song, dance, or larger work.

register: Section of the range of an instrument or voice with a characteristic color. In organ performance, a set of pipes governed by one stop.

rhythm: The element that generates, measures, organizes, and controls musical time.

rondo: A piece built by alternations of refrains and episodes, as in A B A C A D A.

round: A simple type of imitation, in which a number of voices, beginning at different times, sing the same melody over and over again.

sarabande: Rather slow dance in triple time, with an accent of length generally upon the second beat of the measure; Spanish in origin.

scale: A stepwise series of notes, usually denoting a rising line. Scales are qualified according to the arrangement of whole steps and half steps. (See major scale, minor scale, chromatic scale, diatonic scale.)

scherzo: Italian for "joke." A quick, dancelike movement that all but supplanted the minuet in the nineteenth-century symphony.

sharp: A sign (♯) that raises by a half step any note before which it is placed.

signature: The group of sharps or flats and the meter indication of a composition; both are found at the beginning of the piece; the key signature (sharps or flats) is placed at the left of each staff system throughout the piece.

sonata: Italian word meaning "sounded." In the seventeenth and early eighteenth centuries, this term was applied to a three- or four-movement piece for one to four instruments. Later, the term applied to a piece in two or more movements for one or two instruments; the first movement was generally in sonata form.

sonata form: The most important form of the Classic era; basically, a long-range harmonic plan in which each key area has distinctive thematic material. See exposition, development, recapitulation, coda.

staccato: Performed in a markedly detached manner. (See détaché, legato.)

staff: The system of five lines upon which music is notated.

subject: A distinctive melodic statement, generally in a large composition, which will be developed in some fashion after it has been presented.

symphony: The most important orchestral form of the late eighteenth and nineteenth centuries. A three- or four-movement work, of which the first movement is always in sonata form.

syncopation: Shift of accent or length from the normal position occupied by a point of arrival (for example, accenting the second beat rather than the first); it creates imbalance and intensifies movement.

tarantella: A quick Italian dance in $\frac{6}{8}$ time, giguelike.

tempo: Synonym for pace.

texture: The composite action of the component voices or parts performing at any given time; includes monophonic, unison, single action (isometric), melody and accompaniment, imitative and nonimitative polyphony, and give-and-take.

theme: A distinctive melodic statement, usually part of a long movement.

three-part structure: Ternary form (A B A), the important feature of which is some sort of contrasting episode setting off two statements of the principal idea, phrase, period, or larger section.

tonal center: A tone that is given prominence in a phrase, period, or larger section acting as a point of reference, arrival, or stability. This prominence can be given by melodic, rhythmic, or, most strongly, harmonic means.

tone-row: A distinctive pattern using all twelve notes (tones) of the chromatic scale without repetition; this pattern acts as the source material for an entire movement or composition. Developed in the early twentieth century.

tonic: The tonal center, the principal note of a key.

transformation: The technique of altering the character of a theme without destroying its basic shape or identity; frequently used in Romantic music to establish structural unity.

treble: A voice or instrument performing in a high range, such as a treble viol. The high range itself, as applied particularly to choral composition.

triad: A chord of three notes, consisting of a root, third, and fifth (for example, C-E-G).

tritone: The augmented fourth, involving three whole steps, as F to B. The term is also applied to the diminished fifth, since both intervals have a similar function of creating harmonic tension to indicate a tonal center. (See enharmonic.)

two-reprise form: A dance-derived form consisting of two sections or periods; the first ends with an open or inconclusive cadence, the second with a conclusive or closed cadence; material in the two sections tends to be similar.

tutti: The full ensemble in a Baroque instrumental work.

upbeat: A note or group of notes preceding an accented note. The upbeat usually is found immediately preceding the measure line (or bar line).

variation: The alteration or elaboration of one or more features of a subject or theme. Also compositions in which the procedure of variation is the principal means of carrying the structure forward.

woodwind instruments: A family of instruments, constructed of a keyed tube of wood (or metal) and producing sound by the vibration of a reed (or double-reed) in the mouthpiece (with the exception of the flute). In addition to flutes, the family includes clarinets, oboes, bassoons.

ABOUT THE AUTHOR

"MY FIRST AMBITION WAS TO BE A COMPOSER, but I realized in about 1960 that my major interests were musicology, teaching, and writing." So admits Leonard Ratner, all of whose interests are happily allowed expression in his role as professor of music at Stanford. The courses he teaches, especially Introduction to Music and The Beethoven String Quartets, bring him a great deal of enjoyment, and his writings have brought him much acclaim as a musicologist. *The Listener's Art*, first published in 1957, is widely used as a textbook in introductory courses, and *The Classic Style*, published in 1980, is a historical and encyclopedic study of the classic principles of composition. *The Classic Style* is Professor Ratner's major work in the field in which he is recognized as an outstanding specialist, the Classic era of Haydn, Mozart, and Beethoven. It has already become a basic reference book for the Classic period and a model for the study of musical style.

Among his other distinctions, Professor Ratner can claim the first doctorate in music awarded by the University of California at Berkeley. He came to Stanford from Berkeley in 1947 to teach, and was named professor of music in 1957. A Guggenheim Fellow in 1962, he has several times been a visiting lecturer at Bar-Ilan University and the Hebrew University in Israel. His love of travel has been well served, too, by teaching assignments at Stanford overseas campuses in Beutelsbach, Semmering, and Florence.

Although he turned from active musical composition in 1960, Professor Ratner's orchestral compositions have been performed by the New York Philharmonic and the San Francisco and Portland symphony orchestras, and his chamber music by Adolph Baller, Gabor Rejto, and the Walden Quartet. His opera, *The Necklace*, first performed in 1960, enjoyed a successful revival at Stanford in March 1983. On occasion, he appears as combined lecturer/performer; his instrument is the violin.

Coincident with contemporary styles of music, Professor Ratner observes a steady, strong interest in Classic music among his students. "It often surfaces later," he says, "when the students discover that Classic music offers greater challenge and satisfaction, exercises the spirit more than the musical environment they have grown up in."

Professor Ratner lives on the Stanford campus with his wife, Ingeborg, an artist. The Ratners have two daughters: Karen, a physician, and Miriam, a psychologist and family counselor.

CREDITS

INDEX

Exposition:
    in fugue, 99
    in sonata form, 93
Expressionism, 120, 123

Fanfare, 65
Fantasia, 100
Finale, 91
Flute (see Instruments)
Form, 30, 77–101
Fourth (interval), 128
Foxtrot, 29
Fugue, 98–100
Furiant, 29

Galop (dance), 29
Gavotte (dance), 28, 62
Gigue (dance), 29, 62
Give-and-take in texture, 57
Goethe, Johann:
    "The Erlking," 69–71
Gregorian chant, 18, 36, 80

Habanera, 29
Half cadence, 50
Half note, 30, 129
Half step, 129
Handel, Georg Friedrich:
    Concerto Grosso (D Major),
      95
    Concerto Grosso (F Major),
      95
    Messiah, 9, 16, 61
Harmonic color, 10–12
Harmonic instability, 43, 44, 45
Harmonic progressions, 44
Harmonic stability, 43, 44, 45
Harmony, 43–51, 76–80
    in Classic music, 12
    in medieval music, 11
    in Renaissance music, 11
    in Romantic music, 12

in twentieth-century music,
    12
    (*See also* Cadence; Key; Mod-
      ulation; Tonal center)
Harp, 10
Haydn, Joseph:
    Creation, 62, 65
    Quartet in D Major, 58
    Sonata for Piano (D Major),
      91
    Sonata for Piano (E♭ Major),
      22, 23, 74
    Symphony no. 102 (B♭ Ma-
      jor), 16
    Symphony no. 103 (E♭ Major,
      Drumroll), 65, 74, 75
"Home, Sweet Home," 130
Homophony, 53, 54
Honegger, Arthur:
    Pastoral d'Été, 68
Horn (French horn), 11
Hornpipe, 29
Hunt, signal, 65

Imitation, 55
Impressionism, 120
Instruments:
    Brass, 9, 10
      horn, 10
      trombone, 10
      trumpet, 10
      tuba, 10
    percussion, 9
      bells, 10
      celesta, 10
      timpani, 10
    string, 9
      cello (violoncello), 9
      contrabass, 9, 10
      harp, 10
      viola, 9
      violin, 9